Dixie Dean Machine

37 Hattricks For One Club

by

Mark Cuddy

Copyright © 2020 Mark Cuddy

ISBN: 978-0-244-55984-7

All rights reserved, including the right to reproduce this book, or portions thereof in any form. No part of this text may be reproduced, transmitted, downloaded, decompiled, reverse engineered, or stored, in any form or introduced into any information storage and retrieval system, in any form or by any means, whether electronic or mechanical without the express written permission of the author.

www.publishnation.co.uk

Contents

Preface

1. Introduction
2. The Beginning - season 1924/25
3. The First of Many - season 1925/26
4. "He'll Never Play Football Again" - season 1926/27
5. The Unbreakable – season 1927/28
6. Three Hattricks in Eleven Days - season 1928/29
7. Going Down - season 1929/30
8. Smashing Records - season 1930/31
9. Champions Again - season 1931/32
10. Up for the Cup - season 1932/33
11. Broken Bones -season 1933/34
12. Back to the Top of the Pile -season 1934/35
13. Another Broken Toe - season 1935/36
14. Beating Bloomer - season 1936/37
15. The Final Whistle - season 1937/38
16. The Statistics

Bibliography

Preface

In trying to research thoroughly Dixie Dean's 37 hattricks for Everton, I have found conflicting information from different sources on a number of occasions. Not so much on the hattricks themselves but on other incidents that surround the games and goals. For example, in the book 'Everton, The Official Centenary History', it states that Dixie returned from his long lay-off in season 1926-27 with a goal for the reserves in a Central League match at Huddersfield Town on 9th October 1926.

Dean is also quoted in the book 'Dixie Dean, The Inside story of a Football Icon', confirming this moment, "Ted Critchley sent this ball over, I headed it into the back of the net…"

However, The Liverpool Post and Mercury that reported on the game at the time stated his return against Huddersfield was a 3-0 defeat. He did hit the bar with a header from a long free kick but didn't score. Furthermore, Critchley hadn't yet signed for Everton.

Dean did score with a header in his second reserve outing, at Goodison Park in a 3-2 victory over Birmingham City a couple of days later, but once again Critchley couldn't have supplied the cross because he hadn't yet signed for Everton. I can only assume that because Dean scored literally hundreds and hundreds of goals for Everton, over time, especially in his later years, some of the goals and games merged in his memory as one, when he was regaling stories, often off the cuff, of his magnificent career.

Because of these differing accounts, I have tried my best to research from as many sources as possible, especially from newspaper reports following the games themselves, and return my own account from the information available to me.

Introduction

Football fans of every club, filled with passion, appreciation, and a thirst for knowledge for the game, know that Everton's Dixie Dean scored 60 league goals in one season in top flight football, a record that will probably never be broken.

It's an astounding record that was set in season 1927-28, in a time when teams could play one match on one day and the following day have to play another match which could be anywhere in the country, often the reverse fixture.

Sometimes there could be three matches in four days. Example, in season 1927-28, when Dean scored his 60 league goals; Everton played Arsenal away on Christmas Eve, then Cardiff at home on Boxing Day and then Cardiff away the following day, on the 27th December. These types of fixtures were common in these days. In fact, in season 1924-25 Everton played three matches in three days; at home to Newcastle on Christmas Day, away to Newcastle on Boxing Day and at home to Birmingham on the 27th December.

There were twenty-two clubs in the top division, and as well as these games coming thick and fast, they could be played on football pitches that during adverse weather, could become mud-sodden, dangerous, and sometimes scattered with straw to allow a game to be played or continued. Everton's pitch of season 1930/31 was particularly bad, and described before the visit of Southampton on 20th December in the Liverpool Post and Mercury as "gluey and treacherous".

Football pitches up and down the land suffered similar problems and were very problematic to play on. The Sheffield Wednesday pitch on December 31st 1928 sounded like an interesting place to traverse. According to the Daily Post's report, two days later, "The ground was covered with snow, intermixed with sand, but in parts it was slippery, and not conducive accurate play."

Only the fittest and strongest could play in these conditions, and it could take great skill just navigating around the pitch.

The ball itself could be a problem. In adverse weather, the laced ball was infamous for being heavy and rock hard when wet, and could often lead to all manner of injuries. Gordon Watson, who won the league with Everton in 1938/39, recalled, "I think the regulation weight was 28 ounces, but it soaked up the water and would often split your forehead if you headed the lace."

The only thing harder than a wet football was the footballers themselves. Hard men that were allowed to thrive within the rules of the game. Allowed to be physical, in a time where there was no time or place for feigning an injury or rolling around the pitch after a tackle. In an interview in the late 1970's, Dean was clear that, "if a player rolled around in agony on the pitch then, you could be sure he was hurt."

There was no such thing as substitutes either. Injured players would try manfully to continue to the end of a game, sometimes carrying all manner of injuries, not wanting to let their team mates down. Often an injured player would leave the field and then return later or intermittingly for the rest of the game. In certain circumstances, an injured player would just be reshuffled to a different position, to one of a less threat from the attacking team.

Although the pitches could be treacherous, and in some cases the players mere "cloggers", and the ball rock hard when wet, and the football boots unsophisticated, it's fair to say that reading the match reports of the time, some of the players had great skill in what they were doing, not just with the ball, but with their positional sense, intellect and tactical know how. It might seem hard to believe, but they could do things with the heavy cased ball that modern day footballers do with the lighter ball of today. In the match reports there are often great descriptions of players swerving the ball, juggling it, and doing neat tricks with it. Things that when you look at the limited rare and grainy black and white footage from back in the day, seems hard to believe. But it did happen, the players had great skill.

It was a time when footballers often lived in the community of the team they played for, and more often than not they would walk to the ground in and amongst the throng of supporters. There was no hiding place for a poor performance, in a time when you had to give your all for the club that paid your wages. Many a player would be unceremoniously dropped after a poor game or two, disappearing out of the side, then reappearing for a different club two divisions below.

It was also a time before football mangers, when the directors of the club along with the trainer selected the team to play on match day. As for tactics, more often than not it was the players who devised what they were going to do during the match. They were allowed to be free thinking, adapting to different tactics as the game was in flow with many tactics, they'd thought up themselves. Speaking in 1978, Dean said, "One of the most significant factors in today's game as compared with football in the 1920's and 1930's is tactics. There is so much written about how a team should play and what the players should do in a match now, that it's a wonder everyone isn't stifled by the sheer number of words. In my opinion these tactical discussions are very much overdone."

The game was very quick and entertaining. For most of the time the idea was simple; score goals quickly and more than the opposition. This didn't mean it was like school-boy football, with twenty players all running around chasing the ball from one side of the pitch to other. It meant you had to be quick physically and mentally, especially in the early stages of the game. There were very few cases of score lines consisting of 0-0, "bore draws."

Domestically there was only league games and FA Cup games, with the Charity Shield thrown in if you were lucky enough to win the league or the FA Cup on a given year. There was no League Cup matches against lower league clubs or European matches against teams that consisted of postmen, bankers, butchers, bakers and a candlestick maker. The games in the top division were tough.

So, to achieve the amount of goals Dean did is simply amazing. But Dean wasn't just a one or two season wonder. In fourteen seasons at Everton, Dean created many records that will probably never be broken, not just at club level but nationally too. These included, scoring 383 goals in total for Everton, with 349 league goals in 399 league games, and 310 of those goals coming in the top division. Other records at club level that will be near to impossible to break include, 200 league goals in 199 games, 300 league goals in 310 games, scoring 28 FA Cup goals, and 6 goals in the Charity Shield, scoring more than 30 league goals in four seasons, scoring more than 20 league goals in ten seasons, being top goal scorer in most seasons at the club, scoring most league goals in derby matches, and being the youngest player to score a hattrick at Everton.

He was literally the club's goal machine tank. There was even a local paper that portrayed him like this in a running caricature.

On the international scene for England he scored 18 goals in 16 games. He really was a goal machine.

What makes Dean's statistics even more incredible, was the fact he had several serious injuries throughout his career, as well as a motorcycle accident that fractured his skull and broke his jaw bone in two places. The accident was life threatening, he was unconscious for the best part of 36 hours, and needed metal plates inserted in his jaw bone to aid recovery. He was lucky to survive, and the doctors were convinced he would never play football again.

On top of this, just to show how tough and physical the game was back then, he endured a football tackle whilst playing for Tranmere against Rochdale that was so high and severe that he had to have an operation to have a testicle removed. The tackle on him was criminal, and by an ageing player who did it through malice because the young Dean had scored two goals against him, making the player look like the aging mug he was.

Dean was a footballer every boy wanted to be. Almost like a superhero, blasting goal after goal into the oppositions net and he done it with a beaming smile on his face. When he scored a goal there was no aggression in is celebration, no arrogance, no anger at all, just pure jubilation. Something that is missing in the modern game.

He was a true legend of the game in his own lifetime. Quoted while still playing as "the greatest centre forward to ever grace the English game."

When his goalscoring became so well known, there were players who were happy to lose a game as long as Dean didn't score against them. Dean tells a story when a player put two fingers down his shorts to stop him scoring from a corner and was pleased that he'd stopped a goal by Dean, even though the player had inadvertently deflected the ball into his own net.

In amongst all the records Dean broke and the ones he made for himself, there is one that often gets forgotten or overlooked, and yet it is as just as an incredible as his major claim to footballing fame, his sixty league goals in one season. It is also another record that will probably never be broken, not just at Everton, but also in the English game; his record of thirty-seven hattricks for one club.

Dean's 37 hattricks is such an achievement, that if we added up the last thirty-seven Everton hattricks, scored by a multitude of players over the seasons, we would have to go back more than forty years from season 2018-19 to season 1978-79. Yet, Dean scored his thirty-seven hattricks in twelve full seasons. The record is truly phenomenal.

Astonishingly, it didn't end there. In his football career, Dean scored forty-three hattricks in total.

Some people will say that Dean was the greatest centre-forward the English game ever witnessed. Liverpool legend Bill Shankly certainly thought so, saying, "Dixie was the greatest centre forward there will ever be. His record of goal scoring is the most amazing thing under the sun."

Other people will say the greatest centre-forward was Jimmy Greaves, Steve Bloomer, or maybe Arthur Rowley, but the truth is, they were all great centre-forwards who scored bags of goals at different times in the history of the game. If it was a game of Top Trumps then they would all beat each other in one category or another, they all had incredible goal scoring records.

And the statistics themselves can be argued when scrutinised. For example, Greaves scored forty-seven top flight goals more than Dean, but he did it by playing more than one hundred and fifty-plus games. But then Rowley scored even more goals than Greaves, but most of his goals weren't scored in the top flight. There are lots of ways at looking at the statistics of these great goal scorers. The best thing I believe anyone can do is just be grateful the English game witnessed these legends, because that's what they all are. Inspiring the next generation of centre-forwards.

Dean's record of 60 league goals in one season in the English top flight might be beaten one day, unlikely but possible, but what about his record of thirty-seven hattricks for one club? That will take some beating. The legendary Steve

Bloomer scored twenty-one for Derby County, and Jimmy Greaves scored fifteen for Tottenham, as well as thirteen for Chelsea. But no one has come near to thirty-seven hattricks for one club in the English game.

It's time to take a look back to all thirty-seven hattricks, the stories behind them, how they were scored, look at some of the people who helped create them, and see how they effected the seasons of Everton Football Club.

The Beginning

Season 1924-25

William Ralph 'Dixie' Dean arrived at Everton from Tranmere Rovers on transfer deadline day, 16th March 1925 for £3,000. His wages started on £5 per week, rising to £6 per week after his first year, before eventually rising to the statutory maximum basic wage of £8 per week.

The fee Everton paid for him was a lot of money for a footballer, especially one so young, but Dean had shown great promise and big things were expected of him. Furthermore, as founding members of the league, Everton were desperate to save their status in the top division. When Dean put pen to paper Everton sat in 20th position from twenty-two teams.

Everton had a terrible season thus far. In the opening ten games they'd won just one, drew four and lost five, scoring just seven goals and conceding fourteen. They would go on to struggle to score goals, and have periods where they just couldn't get a point. Three times in the season they would lose four games on the trot.

Things needed to change, and with only ten games remaining to save their season and the dreaded drop for the first time in their history they bought 18-year old 'Dixie' Dean. The last thing Everton wanted was to become the tenth team of the twelve founding members to be dropped out of the top division. There was only Everton, Aston Villa and Blackburn Rovers from the original clubs that kicked off the English game back in 1888 who were yet to lose their standing status in the First Division.

Before Dean arrived at Everton, he had been scouted by many football clubs. On one occasion, at a Tranmere away game against Ashington, Bert Cooke, the Tranmere secretary took Dean to St. James' Park, Newcastle United's home ground, and introduced him to representatives from Arsenal, Aston Villa, Birmingham City and Newcastle United. Other clubs who wanted to sign him included Liverpool, Manchester United, Middlesbrough and Chelsea. He was even scouted by the best team in the top division of that period, Huddersfield Town, who won the league in three consecutive seasons from 1923/24 to 1925/26.

Huddersfield Town's achievements shouldn't be overlooked because at the time they were the best team in the land. In the six seasons between 1922/23 to 1927/28, Huddersfield won the league three times, were runner's up twice, once to Everton, and finished third on the other occasion.

But Dean refused to sign for any of the teams offered to him, because he had his heart set on joining his boyhood club. He said, "You see, I was just waiting for one club to come for me and that was Everton. They were the only club I ever wanted to play for. I wouldn't have gone to Liverpool, only Everton. This began from my schooldays. I only used to look for the result of one team in the Echo on a Saturday and that was Everton. I didn't care if Liverpool were licked 10-0. That wouldn't affect me at all. If Everton won, that was fine. If they lost, well, it was a bad day."

Everton themselves had shown interest in signing Dean in January 1924, but Tranmere refused a bid of £2,750, before eventually excepting £3,000.

In the season before he joined Everton, the 5 foot 10 and half inch, eighteen-year old, had scored 28 goals in 28 games for Tranmere in the Third Division in all competitions, with 27 goals coming in the league. In amongst the goals, he also scored three hattricks at Prenton Park. His first senior hattrick came against Hartlepool United in a 4-3 win on 25th October 1924. His second and third arrived later in the season, on February 14th against Barrow in a 4-1 win, and on the 7th March against Rochdale in a 3-1 win.

To put Dean's 27 league goals for Tranmere into context, while he scored 27 goals the rest of the team manged 17 goals between them.

Joining Everton was an ambition of Dean's and a dream come true. His dad took him to watch Everton once when Dean was eight years old and he fell in love with the club. He loved the blue Everton shirt so much that the night before a school football game he would sleep in his school's blue jersey dreaming of playing for Everton.

The Liverpool Daily Post and Mercury tried their best to quell Evertonian's enthusiasm for the signing, "It is hoped the crowd will not make a "god" of Dean. He is very human and has many boy-like touches. It is not so much what he has done as the way he has done it, that has impresses. He is natural footballer with a stout heart, a willing pair of feet and a constitution that will stand him in good stead."

But they weren't to know that Dean would stay at Everton for the next 13 years, and would go on to break every club goal scoring record there was, and create some goal scoring records both at club game and nationally, that will never be broken. Furthermore, he would become more than that, and more than any Evertonian could have wished for when the club signed him.

Dean's debut came on 21st March 1925, just five days after he signed for Everton. There were now only nine games remaining for Everton to save their season. Everton were still third from bottom and only one place off relegation, and they were due to face Arsenal away, who were also in the relegation mire.

It wasn't to be a dream start for Dean as Everton suffered a 3-1 defeat. Matters were made worse when, according to Dean, he scored a header that was incorrectly not given. Dean believed that as the ball went sailing into the top corner, the Arsenal goalkeeper scooped the ball out as it went over the line and quickly threw the ball up field, so the referee was convinced it wasn't a goal, and the "goal" wasn't given.

Everton's goal scorer against Arsenal that day was 21-year old left-winger Fred Kennedy, who had signed only four days before Dean, from Manchester United, and made his debut in the game before the Arsenal match, a 1-0 victory over Notts County at Goodison Park.

It was Kennedy who supplied the cross in Everton's next game, Dean's home debut, at home to Aston Villa, that Dean headed into the net for his first Everton goal, in a 2-0 victory on 28th March.

Sadly, Kennedy would become one of those footballers who could never find his footballing home. After leaving Everton after less than three seasons, he would play for four different clubs in the next five seasons, and never settling at one.

Kennedy's Everton career started very well, scoring three goals in his first ten games at the tail end of season 1924/25. Two of the goals were decisive and both at Goodison Park, in 1-0 victories against Blackburn Rovers on 11 April, and Leeds United on the final game of the season on 2nd May.

The following season, he started in blistering form, scoring seven goals in his first nine games. But just over a year later, his Everton career was over, totalling eleven goals in thirty-five league games.

Dean, on the other hand, after heading in Kennedy's cross in the Aston Villa game would go on to play in the next five games, scoring one more goal, and his first away goal for Everton, which came by way of a tap in, against West Ham United in a 4-1 defeat on 18th April.

Dean nearly scored other goals, including, hitting the bar in a 0-0 draw with Preston North End at Goodison on 13th April, as well as having further chances in the West Ham game, as noted by The Daily Courier report, insisting Dean "missed at least two good chances through hesitancy."

By the end of his brief start to life at Everton, Dean had scored two goals in seven games. Nothing to write home about, but seeing as Everton's top goal scorer was Jimmy Broad, with eight goals in seventeen games, with all his goals scored in fourteen league games, Dean must have known he didn't have too much to do to become next season's top scorer, and he must have already been fixing his sights on the following season.

As for Everton, they finished the season in 17th place, and it was clear why they had signed Dean – they desperately needed to score more goals. At home, only relegated Nottingham Forest scored less goals than Everton's twenty-five goals.

Away from Goodison, only the bottom three clubs, Arsenal and the two relegated teams; Nottingham Forest and Preston North End, scored less than Everton's pitiful fifteen goals from twenty-one games.

An even worse statistic was Everton's one single victory away from home, a 1-0 win against Nottingham Forest on 25th October.

What made matters gruelling for Evertonian's was in the previous season Everton had finished 7th and didn't slip out of the top ten from October to the end of the season. This coming after beating Liverpool home and away in consecutive games, 1-0 at Goodison Park on 6th October, and 2-1 at Anfield a week later.

Everton had the 8th best away record in season 1923/24, and the 4th best home record, losing just once at home to Sunderland on Boxing Day.

Everton also had the league's top goal scorer in Wilf Chadwick. Chadwick hit a total of 30 goals in 44 games, with 28 goals coming in a full league campaign. Behind Chadwick, Everton had Jack Cock who scored 17 goals in 37 games, with 15 goals in the league from 35 games.

If Chadwick and Cock's league goals were added up from season 1923/24, they scored more goals than the entire Everton team put together in season 1924/25. That's how much of a dry spell Everton's forward play was under.

The strange thing was, both Chadwick and Cock played in season 1924/25 but only managed 11 league goals between them. Both got off to a good start too with a goal each, in the first game of the season, a 2-2 draw away at Birmingham City. Chadwick then scored the only goal in Everton's first home game of the season, a 1-0 win against West Bromwich Albion on 6th September.

Unfortunately, after that the goals started to dry up. Everton won just one game in the opening ten, scoring just seven goals, with Chadwick scoring four of them.

The barren spell for the two centre-forwards in season 1924/25 eventually led to their departures. Jack Cock was dropped from the Everton first team to the reserves, after a 3-1 defeat against Liverpool on 7th February, and never played for the first team again. A month later, just days before Dean's arrival, Cock was transferred to Plymouth Argyle in Third Division South, scoring a bucket full of goals, before moving on to Millwall and scoring more goals. At Everton he scored 31 goals in a total of 72 games.

Outside of football, Cock had a remarkable life. Firstly, in the First World War he earned the Military Medal for "Bravery in the Field." And he starred in two films with football in the theme; the silent film 'The Winning Goal' (1920), and the talky 'The Great Game' (1930). A fun-filled packed life.

As for Chadwick, his last goal for Everton also happened to be in that derby defeat at Anfield. He played only eight more games for Everton before moving on to Leeds United the following season.

Chadwick's short time at Everton was interesting and at the beginning it was almost a Roy of the Rover's style storyline. Plucked from the Lancashire Combination league team Rossendale United in February 1922, after scoring 36 goals in 23 games, he was put straight into Everton reserves where he scored two goals on his debut at Anfield in a 3-2 victory. In the next two games he scored twice in each game as Everton beat Derby County 4-1 at home and 4-3 away. Chadwick got his chance in the first team when Bobby Irvine was away on international duties, and he scored both goals in Everton's 2-0 victory against Bradford City at Goodison Park. The reverse fixture, a week later he scored Everton's only goal in a 3-1 defeat. All of this happening to the 21-year old in his first month at Everton.

Unfortunately for Chadwick, two games later when he missed two easy chances in a 1-0 defeat away to Preston North End, he was dropped back to the reserves. He stayed in the reserves until he was recalled to the first team on 14th October, for the Goodison derby. Everton lost 1-0, a week after losing 5-1 also to Liverpool, but Chadwick stayed in the side, and scored a penalty in his next game, a 2-1 defeat against Nottingham Forest. He finished his first full season at Everton as joint top goal scorer, along with Billy Williams, with 13 goals.

The following season he would become the league's top goal scorer with 28 goals, and not miss a single match all season. In total he scored 30 goals, with 2 in the FA Cup, one against Preston North End and the other against Brighton Hove

Albion. Along the way to becoming the division's leading marksman, he would score four goals in a 6-1 win against Manchester City at Goodison Park, and another hattrick against Tottenham Hotspur in a 4-2 victory also at Goodison Park.

In total goals, he would be the top goal scorer for the club again the following season with 9 goals, scoring 6 in the league and 3 in the FA Cup. He was just two league goals behind eventual Everton top league scorer for the season, Jimmy Broad. But by then, his time at Everton was almost up.

At Everton he scored a goal every two games, finishing with 55 goals in total in 109 games. When he moved to Leeds United things didn't really work out for him. But he found success a season later at Wolverhampton Wanderers, before finishing his career on a damp note at Halifax Town.

Before he left for Leeds United, Chadwick must have witnessed the rise of Dean, and watched him begin to pick up the mantle he once held briefly himself. I wonder how he felt?

The First of Many

Season 1925-26

Surprisingly, with the arid season of goals that Everton had endured in season 1924/25, the Everton selectors stuck with Jimmy Broad as their preferred centre forward to start season 1925/26. Broad had scored 5 goals in 8 league games at the end of the previous season. Dean, along with Chadwick, had to settle for the reserves in the Central League.

Unfortunately for Broad, things didn't get off to a good start. He didn't find the net in the opening four games. Everton drew three and lost one. That is not to say Everton started the season poorly, if anything lady luck just wasn't on their side. In the opening game, at home to FA Cup holders Sheffield United, they drew 2-2 with goals from Kennedy and Troup, but they also hit the bar on two other occasions and shot themselves in the foot by giving away two goals, one with a short back pass and the other with a penalty.

In the second game of the season, a 1-1 draw against West Bromwich Albion, the Everton goalkeeper Harland got injured after 15 minutes and had to go off. These were the days before substitutions, so when he went off Everton were down to ten men. Left Back, Jack O'Donnell deputised in goal while the rest of the team shuffled about into a new system. Broad was left up front on his own, waiting and hoping for a chance, and it was his back-heel that gave Irvine the chance to score, and he did and Everton were 1-0 up.

West Brom would go on and equalise but it was a brave display by Everton, and an honest point gained by team work. None more so braver than Harland, hobbling back on to the pitch in the second half with 35 minutes remaining, with an injury that was so constricting that the Liverpool and Daily

Post harshly reported that, "he was materially of little use to his side."

The injury would keep him out of the side for the next six games, and in came reserve keeper Jack Kendall. Harland returned for the derby where Everton lost 5-1 at Anfield, and the following game a 3-2 defeat at home to eventual league champions Huddersfield Town. That game would be Harland's last game for Everton in the first team. The following August, he left the club and joined Runcorn.

Like so many footballers in this period, Harland's career was a mixed bag. Signed from Linfield as a stand-in for the injured Tommy Fern, he made his debut in a 1-0 win over Arsenal at Goodison Park on 4th November 1922. He played the next 19 games keeping 4 clean sheets, before first choice Fern came back into the side. The following season he had to wait until the 5th January before he saw first team football again after Fern was dropped. For the remainder of his career he was in and out of the team for one reason or another, as the selectors chose either him, Kendall, Harry Hardy or reserve keeper and rookie Charles Menham. In total, Harland made seventy appearances for Everton.

Unlike the teams of today where there's a first-choice goalkeeper and a reserve goalkeeper, back in the 1920's the squads were bigger because there was more chance of injury, not just from opposition players but also from the pitches that the games were played on. It was the days when the goalkeeper could be charged, leading to lots of injuries.

During Harland's four full seasons at Everton, six different goalkeepers were used in the first team. In seasons 1925-26 and 1926-27, Everton used four different goalkeepers in the season through either injury or being dropped.

Indeed, Everton bought Harry Hardy from Stockport County in October because Harland and Kendall were both injured. Hardy was thrown straight into the deep end against

Arsenal at Highbury and picked the ball out of the net on four occasions, in a 4-1 defeat.

In the fourteen seasons that Dean was at Everton, there were thirteen different Everton goalkeepers between the sticks. And in only three of those seasons, did Everton manage to stick with the same keeper throughout the campaign, 1928-29 (Davies), 1930-31 (Coggins) and 1932-33 (Sagar).

With Harland injured after the second game, in came Kendall, and in Everton's next game, they lost 2-1 away to Cardiff City. It was a game that Broad as well as a number of Everton players had chances to get something out of the game after going two goals down before half-time. But they failed, and scored a last-minute goal by David J. Murray as a consolation.

In the fourth game of the season, at home to Birmingham City, Broad must have known the gods were against him when after running after the referee to claim a penalty he was accidentally and comically knocked out by the referee waving his arm as if to say "play on."

In a tough game, Fred Kennedy and Alec Troup, just like in the first home game of the season, scored the Everton goals in a 2-2 draw.

Meanwhile, Dean had scored seven goals in the reserves against Bradford City in a 10-0 rout. Dean was restored to the first team and replaced Broad.

It was a tale of two strikers. Dean would finally begin his first full season at Everton, proper, while Broad didn't get near the first team again. After playing a couple of games in the reserves, Broad left for New Brighton in the Third Division North.

Dean joined the first team in the fifth game of the season, at Goodison Park against Tottenham Hotspur on 12th September. It was a free-flowing game that finished 1-1, with the Liverpool and Daily Post suggesting Everton were a little lucky to get a point. They also suggested Dean was prominent in the Everton attacks.

After the Tottenham game, Dean didn't miss a single game for the rest of the season, playing a total of 40 games, 38 in the league and 2 in the FA Cup.

With Dean's inclusion, things didn't automatically or dramatically improve. They won only one game in the next seven, with four defeats and two draws. However, his impact was felt in his second game when Everton got their first win of the season with a 4-0 win against West Bromwich Albion at Goodison on 16th September. Dean supplied three of the passes for the four goals.

Just like the previous season, the results away from home were dreadful. In six games they lost four and drew two, conceding 22 goals along the way. In amongst this run of results away from home they got thrashed 7-3 by Sunderland in a match where Dean scored his second goal of the season.

Dean's first goal of the season came in his third game, in an entertaining 4-4 draw away at Manchester City. But it was after the 7-3 defeat against Sunderland when Dean exploded on the scene, scoring two consecutive hattricks in the space of a week, enabling Everton to claim back to back victories for the first time since January the previous season.

Dean's first hattrick for Everton set a new record that still stands today. Aged 18 years and 268 days, he became the youngest Everton player to score a hattrick in the first team.

The hattrick came away at Burnley, on 17th October, with Dean bagging all the goals by the 78th minute of the game, in a 3-1 win. The ammunition for Dean's first hattrick was mainly down to Alec Troup. This was Burnley's first defeat at home. The game was played at such a pace, that The Daily Courier reported the referee was quoted coming off the field, "It has been one of the fastest games I have refereed."

This may have had something to do with the new offside rule which came into play that season. The new rule, stated that instead of needing two players between the attacker and the goal keeper, you now only needed one player between the goalkeeper and the attacker.

Well after Dean hung up his boots, there have been many theories to why Dean scored so many goals. It's suggested that he profited while teams and the referees came to terms with the new rules. Everton themselves tried a 'W' formation for the game at Burnley, allowing Dean to play further up field, and it payed off. Although the Daily Courier also suggests that the victory was obtained because the, "Everton men also cut out fancy football."

Other suggestions for Dean's goals include the attacker could be more forceful when going for the ball with the goalkeeper. This is true, but the goalkeeper could also take no prisoners, and often the centre-forward was a marked man from the other defenders, if not the rest of the opposition team.

Statistically, there were more goals being scored when the new rule came into play, but neither theory stands up to scrutiny, because if it were so, where were all the other goal scorers? Why weren't they breaking records? Why was Dean more of an exception?

Furthermore, Dean was yet to set the league record, that has yet to be broken, that was still two seasons away. That's two seasons for the referees and defenders to "understand" the new rule. And after Dean created that record of 60 league goals in one season in the top flight, the next best is Aston Villa's Pongo Waring three seasons later, with 49 goals in season 1930/31. That's still eleven goals short of Dean's. And after Waring, who is next in line in the goal scoring charts? Yes, one William Ralph 'Dixie' Dean with 45 goals in season 1931/32.

Dean put his goals down to a number of things. Firstly, he was completely football daft as a kid, and would play football every time he could, anywhere he could, and in any team he could find. He claimed his heading ability was forged when he was a boy, he used to practice his heading at Wesley Hall chapel for hours at a time. Its low roof was used to nod the ball along without it touching the floor. His powerful kicking with both feet was aided when at age fourteen he started to work at the Wirral Railway, and some shifts required him to work at night around the engine shops which were plagued with rats. On seeing a rat, he would quickly run up to it and kick it as hard as he could, imagining it to be a ball.

Also, Dean wasn't a one-man-army, he needed supplies and he always found himself surrounded by great players throughout his Everton career. Not just wingers and inside forwards like Sam Chedgzoy, Bobby Irvine, Ted Critchley, George Martin, Alex Stevenson, Albert Geldard, and Alec Troup who were expert in inch perfect passes of the ball. Dean was supplied from almost every position possible. Cliff Britton, for example, who was more of a right-half. Dean said Britton was like, "A great artist who laid off quite a few goals for me."

Dean knew if it wasn't for the talented players in the team, he wouldn't have scored as many goals as he did. It was a team game and Dean always went out of his way to recognise this and praise his fellow team mates. Dean said the following of Alec Troup, "He and I had an almost perfect liaison. I have to thank Alec as much as if not more than anybody else for helping me to score goals."

As much as the new offside rule aided the attacker, Dean's goals came from hard graft, natural ability, clever positional play, and having the players around him who knew what he needed to succeed in scoring goals. Joe Mercer said of Dean, "He had the ability to stand still until they went for him and then he wasn't there. His temperament was perfect and he also had the knack of using the ball impetus."

The new offside rule certainly helped teams play further up the field in a more attacking sense, and it does seem from the match reports at the time that some players and officials struggled with the new rule, but to suggest this was a major factor in Dean's goal scoring ability doesn't really stand up. There have been many times in the history of the game that there have been peaks and troughs when it comes to goal scoring without any interference from "new rules". Example; seasons 1997-98 and 1998-99 the leading marksmen scored just 18 goals to be the leading league goal scorer. What was the course of that sudden drop from season 1995-96 with 31 goals and season 2000-2001 with 30 goals? That's a drop of twelve and thirteen goals. The same statistic can be found in season 1901-02 with 18 goals, shooting up to 31 goals the following season. In season 1934-35 Arsenal's Ted Drake was top of the pile with 42 goals. The following season there were three players all topping the chart on 31 goals. Two of those players were both at Sunderland. Just peaks and troughs.

There are seasons when the whole league seems to "play safe" away from home. It's a philosophy that still stands today. A point against the champions is a well-earned point. While a point against the team already relegated is two points dropped.

Everton's win against Burnley was convincing, and Dean's performance was described in the Daily Courier as, "Dean was in the picture throughout, enterprising and untiring."

A great success for Dean, the game was also Wilf Chadwick's final game for Everton, before leaving to sign for Leeds United on 17th November.

Within a week of his first hattrick, Dean scored his second, and first at Goodison Park on 24th October, in a 4-2 victory over Leeds United. It was the first time since Wilf Chadwick's three goals in a 4-2 victory over Tottenham in season 1923-24 that an Everton player had scored a hattrick at Goodison.

Dean scored his first goal after three minutes, and two crosses from Chedgzoy either side of half time helped him to complete his hattrick ten minutes after the second half had begun. Chedgzoy also crossed for Kennedy to get the other goal, sandwiched between Dean's second and third goal.

Not surprisingly the Daily Courier picked out Chedgzoy for much praise for Dean's display and goals, and supplying, "Dean with passes along the carpet."

The paper was also a little critical of Everton when the game was won, "Everton might have scored even more goals, but in the last quarter they dropped into their old style. The pretty "me to you, and you to me" passes were introduced."

This was Dean's first consecutive hattrick for Everton, and before his career was over at the club, he would repeat the feat four more times.

The following game, Dean drew a blank in a fog-filled 4-1 defeat away at Arsenal, before scoring five goals in the next four games. Dean should possibly have had a further hattrick when he scored two goals against Notts County away on 14th November. The Liverpool Daily Post reported that, "Chedgzoy on more than one occasion put the ball to Dean for the latter to shoot just wide of the net."

It wasn't just in the league that Dean had a chance for another hattrick. When Everton played Burnley in the second round of the Lancashire Senior Cup, Dean scored two but then blazed a penalty over the crossbar.

Everton's poor start to the season gradually improved, and from 14th November to Boxing Day, Everton went on an eight-game unbeaten run, winning four and drawing four, with Dean scoring nine goals in that spell.

During that period, Dean recorded a further hattrick, away at Newcastle United on 12th December, in a 3-3 draw. On the same day, Hughie Gallacher made his debut for Newcastle and scored two goals.

Like Dean at Everton, Gallacher was to become a legend himself at both Newcastle and for Scotland, and at other clubs he played for, including Chelsea, Derby County and Notts County, he had a very impressive goal scoring record. At Newcastle United he scored an incredible 143 goals in just 174 games. When Dean had finished his football career, he declared that along with Tommy Lawton, Gallacher was, "The finest centre-forward I've ever seen." High praise indeed.

For the record, on a different occasion, Dean also said the greatest all-round player he ever saw was Everton's very own T.G. Jones, the player christened the Prince of Centre Halves.

Newcastle had never been a happy hunting ground for Everton. Since the first away match on 7th Jan 1899, Everton had only beaten Newcastle away three times in twenty-three games.

On this occasion, although Everton might not have come away with all three points the performance was described by the Daily Courier as, "a feat of which the team has every reason to be proud" and suggested the Newcastle locals thought Everton had "put up the best show that has been seen on the ground this season."

As for Dean's hattrick, he scored the opening goal of the game in the 9th minute from a cross by Troup. Newcastle then went 3-1 ahead, which the Daily Courier reported, "It could be said with truth the lead was undeserved and that the Blues had fully as much of the game as their rivals."

Dean scored Everton's second, five minutes after Newcastle's third goal and added one more near the end of the game. Everton had played well and the draw was the least they could have asked for. The Daily Courier reported that Dean's finishing was excellent and the Newcastle goalkeeper, "had no chance at all with any of the three goals against him."

Although Everton's away record at Newcastle was poor, at Goodison in league and FA Cup games they'd won 14, drew 2 and lost 9. And when 24th April came around, Everton added another victory against them, all courtesy of Deans fourth hattrick of the season, in a 3-0 victory. The score line was a replica of the score line of the first time the two teams met at Goodison on 10th September 1898.

In between the two games against Newcastle, Dean scored thirteen goals, and could have had more with better finishing. On 17th March he scored two goals against Sunderland in a 2-1 win, but should have scored a hattrick. The Daily Courier pointed this out in their match report, "Both Batten and Dean missed open goals."

His second hattrick of the season against Newcastle United, came at Goodison Park in Everton's last home game, and the penultimate game of the season. Just four months after his last hattrick. He became only the second Everton player to score a hattrick against the same club in the same season. The other was Bert Freeman in season 1908-09, when he scored two hattricks against Sheffield United in two, 5-1 victories.

In the Newcastle game, the Daily Courier waxed lyrical about Dean's performance, "A feature of the closing game at Goodison Park was the triumph of Dean… He proved himself a centre of skill and strength ready to give and take a charge. His positional play was splendid."

Dean's first goal came from a corner kick from Chedgzoy in the 14th minute. It was Everton's fourth corner of the game. The Liverpool Echo described the header as, "Dean glided the ball."

His second and third goal were aided by passes from Reid and Troup. The report in the Daily Courier, sounded like terrific goals, and worthy of the paper's eulogies, "The young centre nodded the ball on, then raced up regained it, and released an unerring first time shot. Dean's third goal, however, was the pick of the basket for after Troup had given him the ball, he had to swerve away from Chandler and then shoot."

It is worth noting that only a few days before the Newcastle game at Goodison Park, Everton kindly played a benefit match away at Plymouth Argyle for Patsy Corcoran, where Dean scored a hattrick in a 4-3 win. The Daily Courier reported, "Dean, gave a dexterous exhibition of the ball control."

By the end of his first full season, Dean had scored four hattricks, and scored thirty-three goals in forty appearances in all competitions. Thirty-two of the goals came in the league and the other goal came in a disappointing FA Cup campaign, going out at the first hurdle in a replay to Fulham, who were in the Second Division and would finish fourth from bottom.

On the plus side for Dean, he didn't miss a game from the moment he was brought into the side on 12th September. He also hit a hot streak from 10th October to Christmas Day, scoring seventeen goals in twelve games. Dean's goals were a highlight in an otherwise forgettable season.

To put Dean's goal tally into context, up until season 1925-26, only two other Everton players had scored more league goals in one season; Bobby Parker scored 36 league goals, with 38 goals in total in all competitions, in 1914-15, and Bertie Freeman scored 38 league goals in 1908-09, which at the time itself had broken the league record for most goals in a season.

Apart from Bobby Parker and Bertie Freeman, only four other Everton players have ever equalled or bettered Dean's first full season tally; Tommy Lawton scored 38 goals in all competitions, with 34 in the league, in 1938-39, John Willie Parker scored 33 goals in all competitions, with 30 in the league, in 1953-54, Fred Pickering scored 37 goals in all competitions, with 27 in the league, in 1964-65, and Gary Lineker scored 40 goals in all competitions, 30 in the league, in 1985-86 season.

In other seasons, other Everton players came close. Memorably, Bob Latchford was one short of Dean's tally, scoring 32 goals in all competitions, with 30 in the league, in 1977-78.

On the hattrick side of things, Dean's four in his first full season for Everton equalled Bert Freeman's record of most hattricks in a first full season. And Dean was only two hattrick's away from the club record of six hattricks in a season, set by Bobby Parker in season 1914/15.

Freeman would go on to collect a further two hattricks in his Everton career, which would take him to joint third place of hattricks for Everton, with six hattricks, along with Fred Geary (1889/90 – 1894/95), and Tony Cottee (1988/89 - 1994/95).

Dean still had to score a further three hattricks to catch Bobby Parker's club record of seven hattricks, but after just one full season he was more than half way there to fulfilling this. Not to forget, he had just set a new record in his first season that is yet to be broken, becoming the youngest player to score a hattrick for Everton.

As for Everton, they finished the season in 11th position. They would hover around mid-table for most of the season. Most of the damage had been done in the earlier part of the season, when they won one game in the first eleven matches, a 4-0 win against West Bromwich Albion at Goodison Park. In the following game, a 4-4 draw against Manchester City, who became one of the teams along with Notts County that got relegated that season, they lost four matches on the bounce, with two heavy defeats away, with Liverpool smashing five past them at Anfield, and Sunderland going two better and smacking Everton 7-3.

From the 17th October to Boxing Day, Everton recovered a bit, only losing two games in twelve matches, and winning six. At home they only lost three matches all season but they drew too many, nine in total. But for the emergence of Dean and his goals, there wasn't much to celebrate from the season if you were an Evertonian. But with Dean in the first team, things were looking up on the goal scoring front.

"He'll Never Play Again"

Season 1926-27

With Dean scoring four hattricks in his first full season at Everton, and finishing the season as top goal scorer with thirty-three goals in forty appearances, with thirty-two goals coming in the league from just thirty-eight appearances, Evertonian's understandably were excited and expecting big things from him in his second full season. However, before the season began, and just a little over six weeks after scoring his last hattrick, Dean was involved in a motorcycle accident that was so severe it not only almost finished his football career but also nearly ended his life at 19 years of age.

The accident occurred on Sunday 10th June 1926 on a short trip out to the North Wales countryside. Travelling with a girlfriend, Evelyn Jones, Dean was involved in a head-on collision with a motorcycle-sidecar combination on St. Asaph Road, Holywell.

According to Dean he crashed through the windscreen breaking his jaw in two places, broke his cheekbone and fractured his skull. He spent the best part of the next 36 hours unconscious, and was lucky to be alive.

Because of Dean's quick thinking just before the impact, he managed to turn the bike allowing Evelyn to be pushed off the bike. This left her with only minor injuries, and she was discharged the following day. As for Dean, his injuries were life threatening.

So severe were Dean's injuries, that the doctors didn't think he would make it. He had to have metal plates inserted into his jaw to aid recovery. When Dean's health did improve, the Everton club doctor James Baxter, was convinced and forecast Dean would never be able to play football again.

On the 9th July, just under a month after the accident the Lancashire Evening Post reported that the following day, Dean had been moved from the Holywell Hospital and transferred to a nursing home in Liverpool. This was the Robert Davies Nursing Home on Eaton Road in West Derby. They also quoted him as saying, "I have been playing a mouth-organ to get my jaw bones in trim."

The quote showed the true character of Dean, which others have testified he had. He must have needed a good sense of humour because in April the Everton Directors changed his contract, stipulating he must abstain from driving or riding a motor bike or a motor bike combination.

It is incredible to believe that after one hundred and twenty-one days after the accident that threatened his life, Dean was in the starting line-up for Everton reserves in the Central League game away at Huddersfield on 9th October. Everton lost 3-0 but Dean had come through the match, was finding his confidence again and hit the woodwork with a header.

Four days later on 13th October he was in the next Everton reserve game, this time at Goodison Park against Birmingham. In only his second game back, he scored two goals in Everton's 3-2 victory, one of the goals was a header and the other from the penalty spot.

Excitement amongst Evertonian's grew when it was reported in The Liverpool Post and Mercury the following day that Dean was in contention for a return to the first team in their next fixture at home to Newcastle United. As it turned out, Dean had an ankle problem and had to miss the game. He was sorely missed and Everton were defeated 3-1. However, he did return in the next league game away at Leeds United.

Everton hadn't won away from Goodison Park yet, but things were about to change, Dean helped them secure a 3-1 win, and helping himself to his first goal of the season in his first match.

In Dean's absence Everton had started the season abysmally and were bottom of the league after thirteen games. This win, was only their second win of the season, with the other coming against Liverpool at Goodison Park by a single goal scored by Jack O'Donnell. Up until the Leeds game, Everton had played six away matches and lost the first five, drawing their last game 3-3 against Blackburn Rovers.

At Goodison Park, they started with a 3-0 defeat against West Ham United, followed by a 0-0 against West Bromwich Albion, before Leicester City beat them 4-3. The win against Liverpool was followed by two draws, a 2-2 against Bury and a 0-0 with Huddersfield Town and then the 3-1 defeat by eventual league winner's Newcastle United.

Everton had played thirteen times, lost eight, including the first five games, and drawn four games. In the first eight games alone, they'd lost seven and drew one. Along the way, there was the usual hard luck stories. On the opening game of the season, against Tottenham Hotspur, the Daily Courier reported, "Everton played delightful football at White Hart-Lane, and the defeat was the result of sheer hard luck."

But to suggest the results were mainly down to bad luck would be masking the truth, they were just very poor at the start of the season. The best example being; when 3-0 up at half-time against Leicester City, they managed to lose 4-3. And during these first six games of the season they played West Bromwich Albion, one of the teams that would be relegated at the end of the season, and they lost 3-2 away and drew 0-0 at home.

Furthermore, the team had struggled to score goals, whilst at the same time couldn't stop letting them in at the other end. In the thirteen games before Dean's return, six Everton players had managed to score fourteen goals between them whilst the team had conceded thirty goals.

But with what Dean had been through, football showed itself to be where it is in the grand scale of things; life WAS and always will be more important than football.

Missing the first thirteen games of the season would have put a dent in any centre-forwards goal scoring record, coupled with how poor the team were playing, it's incredible to think that before the season was over Dean would score twenty-one league goals in only twenty-seven league games, and three goals in four FA Cup matches.

A season's total of twenty-four goals in thirty-one games is a more than decent rate by any centre-forward's standards. The twenty-one league goals came from an Everton team total of sixty-four league goals. It's hard to believe that what Dean had been through, for the second season running, he finished up the club's top goal scorer. Even better, Everton somehow avoided relegation to the Second Division.

More amazingly, less than eight months after the horrific accident which threatened his life, Dean was called up to play for England.

His first international cap came against Wales, at the Racecourse Ground, Wrexham, on 12th February, and it took him ten minutes to register his first international goal. A second goal followed in the 58th minute, in an entertaining 3-3 draw.

But it was on 2nd April 1927 when he made an even bigger impact on the international scene, in front of more than 111,000 spectators at Hampden Park. In only his second international game he scored both goals as England defeated Scotland 2-1.

Scotland led 1-0 through Alan Morton before Dean equalised with a thunderbolt from thirty yards, in the 65th minute. His second goal and the winner, came in the 88th minute. It was England's first win on Scottish soil for twenty-three years. Since the first fixture began in 1872, including friendlies, it was only England's fourth win on Scottish soil in twenty-four games.

Before the end of season 1926-27, Dean made five appearances for England and scored twelve goals, including two hattricks, one against Belgium in a 9-1 thrashing and the other against Luxembourg in a 5-2 victory. The other two goals of the twelve came against France in another 6-0 beating. All twelve goals came between 12th February and 12th May.

As for his return to the Everton first team, Dean followed the goal against Leeds, with another goal in the next game, another 3-1 win, this time against Arsenal at Goodison Park. He scored six goals in his next seven games. Everton won three of those games, drew two and lost two. After these seven games, they then went on another slump, but at least they were now finding the back of the net. After two blanks, Dean would score nine goals in five games.

In amongst those goals, came his lone hattrick for the season, on Christmas Day, at home against Sunderland in a 5-4 win. It was only Dean's tenth game back after his return. It would be the first, but not the last time he would score four goals in a game for Everton.

The Christmas Day victory was a welcome relief for Everton who hadn't won a game in six weeks. December was to be a terrible month for Everton. Burnley and Aston Villa both smashed five goals against them and they lost to Cardiff City at home 1-0 and finished the month off by getting beat 3-2 in the reverse fixture against Sunderland just two days after the Christmas Day victory.

Everton were in such disarray before the visit of Sunderland that they made four changes to the team. After the game they would drop goalkeeper Davies, to which the Liverpool Football Echo put down to, "owing possibly to his faulty handling of a corner kick that made the score 4-4."

The Liverpool Football Echo also suggested that although "Dean's quartet was a fine effort" and "his heading was delicious", the Sunderland goalkeeper should have done better and the only Everton goal not scored by Dean, a goal from Bobby Irvine, was, "the best goal of the match."

But the game was most memorably for being an excellent debut of Ted Critchley, supplying all four crosses for Dean's goals.

Critchley would go to be a great servant for Everton. Signed from Stockport County for £2,500, to replace the Everton stalwart Sam Chedgzoy who had left the club the previous May, Critchley would go on to play 230 games for Everton and scored 42 goals. Picking up two First Division titles in 1927-28 and 1931-32, and one Division Two title in 1930-31.

Critchley had big boots to fill because Sam Chedgzoy was a legend at the club. Signed in 1910, Chedgzoy would stay with Everton until the end of season 1925/26. The Ellesmere Port born Chedgzoy, played 300 games, 279 in the league, and scored 36 goals, with 33 coming in the league. Picking up a Division One league title in 1914-15 along the way, and a Division One runner up with Everton in the 1911-12 season.

Chedgzoy went down in folk lore by changing one of the laws of the game.

The story goes that the Liverpool sports reporter Ernest Edwards, offered Chedgzoy £2 to experiment with a law of the game that had a flaw to it. The law stated that a goal could be scored direct from a corner kick, but did not stipulate if the player taking the corner kick could touch the ball more than once.

So, when Everton played Arsenal at Goodison on 15th November 1924, from a corner kick, Chedgzoy dribbled the ball into the box and shot, to the amazement of the players and the referee. The ball didn't go into the net, but the referee and Chedgzoy spoke about the flaw in the law. Within 48 hours of the final whistle of the game, the FA changed the rules, so that the player taking the corner kick could only strike the ball once.

Apart from the capture of Ted Critchley, and Dean's return, the season for Everton was one to forget. Surviving relegation by four points, Everton ended the season on 34 points and conceded 90 goals. Everton couldn't even beat West Bromwich Albion, one of the two clubs that finished below them, losing 3-2 away and drawing 0-0 at home. Everton, did however beat Leeds United, the other team that finished below them, in Dean's return game back in October, and beating them 2-1 at Goodison Park in March.

The Christmas Day win against Sunderland was an important win and their first since beating Derby County at home 3-2 on 13th November. In a run of five games between these two matches, Everton lost four and drew one, with two heavy defeats away from home against Aston Villa, losing 5-3, and a 5-1 defeat to Burnley.

It wasn't just Aston Villa and Burnley that embarrassed Everton this season, Bury and Bolton Wanderers also scored five against Everton. Leicester City beat them 6-2 and Newcastle United went one better with a 7-3 win. Sheffield Wednesday also beat them 4-0 and Leicester beat them 4-3 at Goodison.

To add more embarrassment, Everton went out of the FA Cup after extra time against Second Division Hull City, after two replays. Hull finished the season 7th in the Second Division.

Apart from escaping relegation by the skin of their teeth, the 5-4 Christmas Day victory over Sunderland, the rise of Critchley, and a 1-0 win over Liverpool at Goodison, Evertonian's had one other thing to celebrate at the end of season 1926-27; Dixie Dean's good health.

It's fair to say that if Dean, hadn't have been injured this season, the season wouldn't have been so bad for Everton. In the fifteen league games he didn't play this season, Everton won one, drew five and lost nine. In the other twenty-seven games in which Dean was in the team, Everton won eleven, drew five and lost twelve. The only two league games he missed after his return were because he was on international duty. During those games, both away from Goodison Park, Everton lost 1-0 to Liverpool and drew 0-0 with Derby County.

Who knows, maybe there would have been more than the one Everton hattrick to add to his tally, after all the following season would be Dean's most explosive, ground-breaking, and the season he would be immortalised as a footballing legend.

As the curtain came down on the season, Dean was just one hattrick behind the other Everton hattrick heroes from the past, Bert Freeman and Fred Geary. He was also just two behind the club's record hattrick hero, Bobby Parker. Within seven months of season 1926/27 ending, Dean would be Everton's record hattrick scorer. And within twelve months of the end of season 1926/27, Dean would already be untouchable with twelve club hattricks, double Freeman's, Geary's and eventually Cottee's.

Unbreakable

Season 1927-28

Season 1927-28 holds a very special season in Everton's history, and especially Dixie Dean's too. This was the season Dean scored the legendary sixty league goals in a season and Everton won the league for the third time.

60 LEAGUE GOALS
Dean achieved 60 league goals in 39 appearances. Since then, the only player to get close to it was Pongo Waring, and he was still eleven away from equalling it. In total Dean scored 63 goals in 41 games for Everton in season 1927-28.

63 GOALS IN 41 GAMES
These two statistics are highlighted because they are simply incredible, and it's fair to say, they may never be broken by anyone.

It might seem unjust to compare the modern-day Premier League game to the old First Division game of the mid 1920's, because they are worlds apart. For a start season 1927-28 contain four more games than the present one, but if we did compare them statistically, at least for a bit of fun, to put Dean's sixty league goals into perspective, in the last twenty years from season 1999/2000 to season 2018/19, collectively Everton players have only scored sixty goals or more in a season on three occasions. In 2009-10 they scored 60 goals, in 2013-14 they scored 61 goals, and in 2016-17 they scored 62.

Of Dean's sixty league goals, only one goal came from the penalty spot. And in this one season alone, Dean would break both Bobby Parker's Everton record of scoring six hattricks in a season (1914/15), and equal Bobby Parker's club career record of seven hattricks, and help to create another record that no Everton player is likely to ever equal or beat; 7 hattricks in 1 season.

Dean started the season off on fire, scoring every time in the first eight games, scoring twelve goals in total. In those opening eight games he scored a brace in four of them; Birmingham City and Huddersfield at home, and Newcastle United and Tottenham Hotspur away. In between the goals against Newcastle and Huddersfield he also scored four goals for the Football League in a match against the Irish League, with the Football League winning 9-1. The four goals were scored in the first twenty-nine minutes of the game.

In the ninth game of the campaign, Dean scored his first hattrick of the season, as Manchester United were put to the sword before half-time at Goodison Park on 8th October. Dean scored all five goals in a 5-2 victory, and scored four of the goals in the first half.

With achieving this feat, Dean set up two mini club records that possibly will never be beaten; one, a single player scoring four goals against Manchester United before half-time, and two, a single player scoring five goals in one game against Manchester United.

Although this was the first time Dean had scored five goals in a game, it wouldn't be the last time he done it. He would go on to score five goals in a game twice again, and in the same season, season 1931-32, but more of that later.

His five goals against Manchester United were of such quality that the Daily Courier reported, "Dean's placing was to an inch, and with the exception, possibly of one, no goalkeeper could have stopped them…Dean manipulated the ball with skill and judgement, and shot with power and precision."

The goal rush started with Everton's first attack, in the second minute. A cross from Critchley to Dean, and it was 1-0. The Liverpool Echo reported that Dean scored the goal in "magnificent fashion". The Critchley and Dean partnership were at it again in the 9th minute, and his hattrick was completed in the 30th minute. He scored a further goal in the 43rd minute, and his fifth on the hour mark, as Everton were rampant. Five goals in sixty minutes. The Liverpool Echo also suggested Dean could have scored more goals as Everton bombarded the Manchester United goal in the last twenty-five minutes of the game, but for the heroics of the Manchester United goalkeeper Lance Richardson who made some great saves to keep the score down.

At the end of the game Lance Richardson was quoted as saying, "Dean is far away the best centre forward I've ever met."

And who was to argue?

This was the first time an Everton player had scored so many goals in a single First Division game since Jack Southworth scored six goals in a 7-1 hammering of West Bromwich Albion on 30th December 1893.

No other Everton player apart from Dean and Southworth has ever scored 5 goals in a top flight game. Tommy Eglington did score five goals in a Second Division game for Everton at home against Doncaster in a 7-1 victory on 11th April 1952, and Bob Latchford also scored five goals, in an 8-0 victory against Wimbledon in the League Cup at Goodison on 29th August 1978, but neither were in the top flight.

But that's not to take anything away from either Eglington or Latchford. Both players were excellent and became club legends during their time at Everton. It is only to illustrate that no Everton player has ever scored five league goals in a game in the top flight. Some have come close with four goals, but none have scored five in a top flight game.

Dean's second hattrick in this magical season came only two weeks after the first, this time away against Portsmouth on Saturday 29th October, where he scored all three goals in a 3-1 victory. Dean was closely marked throughout the game, and showed his true strength, with the Daily Courier reporting that the Portsmouth players did everything to stop him getting on the score sheet, "They threw themselves at the Everton leader in a manner, which would have knocked the heart out of many centre-forwards, but not so "Dixie." He never lost his temper but kept pegging away manfully, and in the end tired out the opposition and finished the afternoon with the "hat-trick" to his credit."

The Liverpool Echo confirmed the Portsmouth players tactics of trying everything they possibly could to stop Dean from scoring. In the build up to the first goal they reported Dean ignored a "bump in the back by a charging defender."

Dean's first goal also showed that although he was famous for scoring goals with his head, he was also good with his feet. Collecting the ball on the half way line, he went charging towards the Portsmouth goal swerving this way and that, avoiding challenges meant to put him off his stride, before putting the ball beyond the out-rushing goalkeeper. The goal, scored just before half time, was an equaliser to the Portsmouth goal that was scored in the 37th minute. His second came from a rebound off the goalkeeper from three yards out after he'd seen his initial header from a cross by Critchley saved. The hattrick was completed five minutes later after great dribbling skills by Weldon, and even though he was tripped, he put in a cross to Dean who according to the Liverpool Echo "scored with an oblique shot." By the end of the game, Dean had scored his 20th league goal in 11 games.

The victory enabled Everton to go top of the league for the first time this season. It was only the second time Everton had played Portsmouth. The first time was in 1903 in the FA Cup were Everton won 5-0.

The following week, Dean scored another hattrick. This time it was at Goodison Park on Saturday 5th November, against Leicester City in a 7-1 mauling against a very good

Leicester side, who would finish third in the table, and beat Everton 1-0 in the return fixture.

When the season ended, Leicester had the best home record of any team in the top flight, losing just two matches, winning fourteen and drawing five. They scored 66 goals at home, six more than Everton. But it was probably their away form that done the damage, only winning four games all season and losing ten and drawing seven. The 7-1 thrashing being a good case in point. Unlike Leicester, Everton on the other hand, had the best away record in the division and only the fifth best at home.

This was Dean's first consecutive hattrick of the season, and his 23rd goal of the season, and it was still only Bonfire Night. One more consecutive hattrick would follow, in the last two games of the season.

The game was dead and buried at half-time with Everton 5-0 up. Dean scored his first in the 24th minute through unselfish work by Troup. Clean through Troup had a chance to score but decided to put it on a plate for Dean who headed into the empty net. Either side of this goal, Weldon scored two goals. His first came after only two minutes and his second a minute after Dean's. Troup scored in the 31st minute before Critchley got the fifth in the 41st minute. In the second half Leicester pulled one back before Dean scored a second in 65th, ghosting between two Leicester players after a pass from Critchley. The hattrick was completed in the 80th minute, which the Liverpool Echo described as the best of the three, "Dean trapped O'Donnell's big clearance without a moment's hesitation and crashed the ball into the net."

It was a fine performance by Dean, with The Liverpool Post and Mercury reporting that Dean had, "demonstrated his wonderful skill as a leader. His deadly shooting, clever distribution, and all-round effectiveness made him an outstanding figure."

In the following match, Dean scored two goals in a 3-0 win away at Derby County, but should have scored more than the brace he did, hitting the post on one occasion and spurning several good chances to score yet another hattrick.

At the end of November, in between his twenty-seven league goals in fifteen games, Dean managed to score four more goals in a 5-3 win, in a charity match assembled of players from the football league, against Blackpool, for the benefit of the Fleetwood District fund.

The fourth hattrick of the season, and his second away from home came against Aston Villa in a 3-2 victory on Saturday 10th December. This shouldn't have come as a surprise to anyone because Dean couldn't stop scoring against Aston Villa. After opening his Everton account against them, a goal at Goodison in a 2-0 victory on 28th March 1925, he would go on to score six goals against them in his next five appearances. And in his first seven games against Aston Villa he scored eleven goals against them.

Although Everton won 3-2, The Daily Courier suggested that they were lucky to do so as their goal was "fortunate not to be beaten in the closing stages, when the Everton goal was overwhelmed."

It was further suggested that the Aston Villa goalkeeper should have done better with all three goals. In the 10th minute of the game, the goalkeeper fumbled a shot from Dean, allowing Dean to knock the ball out of the goalkeeper's hands, and scoring with ease. Then in the 18th minute, after Critchley had hit the crossbar, the goalkeeper knocked the ball down, allowing Dean to knock the ball into the goal quickly. The hattrick was completed with five minutes remaining, when from a long ball by Critchley, Dean spotted the shadow of the goalkeeper racing out, so he back headed the ball over him and into the empty net.

From the hattrick against Aston Villa, to his next hattrick, Dean played twelve matches and scored thirteen goals. In five of those games he scored a brace against Cardiff City, Sheffield Wednesday, Blackburn Rovers, Middlesbrough and Arsenal. He also scored five goals for England against the "Rest" in an international trial at Middlesbrough on the 8th February.

Dean's fifth hattrick of the season, came away at Anfield, in a 3-3 draw on 25th February. It was a game Everton squandered a 3-1 lead in a match the Daily Courier described as, "Merseyside has never seen a keener and more wonderful "Derby" game than that at Anfield since their inception in the season 1894-95", and the game felt like a "full-blooded cup-tie."

Dean scored two goals in the first half. The first came in the 17th minute from a clever bit of play and pass from Weldon, before Dean smashed the ball passed the outward rushing Liverpool goalkeeper. Although Dean was closely marked throughout the game, he scored his second goal in the 40th minute, giving Everton a 2-1 lead at half-time.

When the game resumed, Dean completed his hattrick on the hour mark, and in doing so he equalled the First Division record set by Eddie Harper for Blackburn Rover's, set in season 1925/26.

Nick Walsh in his book about Dean states, that every time Dean scored against Liverpool on this day, he turned to the Kop and bowed like a matador.

I for one, can't think of a better way to celebrate a goal. I don't think it's ever been done better. Evertonian's have celebrated watching Bob Latchford doing a jump and knee tuck, Tim Cahill boxing the corner flag, Duncan Ferguson removing his jersey and showing everyone his muscles and Everton inspired tattoo, several players have skidded on their knees, several players have done a pre-rehearsed shuffle or dance, other players have pointed at their name on the back of the jersey, players have pointed to the sky and thanked their god, while Andy Johnson told everyone it was now 3-0 to Everton, but to simply bow like a matador is poetic and beautiful.

Although Everton would go on to throw away a win at Anfield, the 3-3 draw was a welcome return after a terrible run of three heavy defeats. First, they were knocked out of the FA Cup 4-3 away at Arsenal, Dean got two of Everton's three goals. Then they lost 4-1 away to Huddersfield and then they got hammered 5-2 at home by Tottenham Hotspur. A game in which Tottenham's Eugene "Taffy" O'Callaghan scored four goals.

The 3-3 draw was followed by five winless games; three draws and two defeats. It's hard to believe with the set of results either side of this 3-3 game that Everton would go on to win the league. But they did.

In the final eight games of the season Everton won six and drew two, scored twenty-four goals, with fifteen of those goals coming from Dean. It's another statistic that seems unreal; 15 goals in 8 games, at the end of the season too. Bizarrely, Dean even managed to miss a penalty in a 1-1 draw against Bury at Goodison Park.

The sixth hattrick came in the penultimate game of the season, away at Burnley on 28th April, in a 5-3 victory where Dean scored four goals, and Everton clinched the league. Surprisingly, in the reverse fixture, a 4-1 win for Everton, Dean never scored.

Dean scored after just thirty seconds of the game. After a passing move from Martin to Weldon, Dean forced his way past two defenders before scoring in the far corner of the goal. His second goal came in the 23rd minute from a pass from Troup, which the Liverpool Echo described the goal as, "Wonderful."

His third came five minutes later in the 28th minute. From the Liverpool Echo report, it sounded like a tremendous team goal, "Hart, Cresswell, Martin, Critchley and Weldon passed and passed again, with the Burnley defenders rushing here and there in an endeavour to capture the elusive ball. But before they could do so, Dean had it in the net."

The description shows again that there was more to the game of the 1920's than hoof-ball and bluster.

Dean scored his fourth goal in the 63rd minute. Along with his second goal, which the Liverpool Echo described, after a sweeping Troup pass, that Dean moved "after it like a flash", the fourth goal demonstrated how quick Dean could be and that he was more than just a "traditional centre-forward." Again, the Liverpool Echo reported that after a pass from Critchley, "Dean went after it like a whippet."

With three goals needed to reach the magical sixty and to set a new record, and with only one game left to do it, it was still a tall order.

Dean's final hattrick of the season, in an entertaining 3-3 draw with Arsenal at Goodison on 5th May 1928, will go down as one of those moments every Evertonian wished they'd witnessed for themselves.

Arsenal took the lead after two minutes. But Dean equalised a minute later from a corner by Critchley, which George Martin helped to turn Dean's way. His second came by a penalty in the 5th minute, when he was tripped running into the box.

Nick Walsh describes this magnificently in his book about Dean, "Dean took the ball and placed it on the spot. Silence descended over the ground as though every single one of the 60,000 spectators had been temporarily transfixed, that all life had been extinguished by some supernatural force: an eerie silence, breathless yet electric in its intensity, inert like a fuse ready to be ignited. Dean ran up to take the kick. The fuse was burning and suddenly the vast arena exploded with a deafening roar. The ball was in the back of the net."

The hattrick was completed in the 82nd minute from a corner by Troup, with Dean heading in from a crowded penalty area.

The roar from the ground was supposed to be heard miles away, as far as the docks. Every player, including the Arsenal players shook Dean's hand at the milestone. Very sportsmanlike. That is except the Arsenal player, Charlie Buchan, who was playing his final game of his career and thought the day was about him. How bitter. But it just shows how players tried their hardest to stop Dean scoring. To stop him scoring, regardless of the result, was an individual achievement.

To be fair to Buchan, later in life he explained, "There are many who believe that Arsenal sat back and allowed Dean to get the three goals that broke the record. I can assure them that nothing is farther from the truth. For myself, I wanted to go out on a winning note – just as I came in, back in 1910. The Arsenal players wanted to help me in this by beating the champions. It was a memorable day one I shall remember as long as I live. Dean was then at the height of his powers. When he got the third, the Goodison Park crowd rose to him. It was a scene beyond description."

Dean believed that after he created the league record, other teams especially went out of their way to stop him and the other players from reaching such heights again, "We had a succession of cartilage troubles, fractured bones, broken shoulder blades and so on."

Near the end of the game, Dean asked the referee if he could leave the pitch, which the referee allowed him to. In the dying minutes of the game Arsenal equalised, but that didn't matter. Dean had done it, broke the league record of 59 goals set in the Second Division by George Campsell the season before. Dean had become a football LEGEND, and he was still only twenty-one years of age.

Everton finished the season not just as league champions but also scored more than 100 league goals for the first time in their history; 102 league goals to be exact. As well as Dean's sixty league goals, Dean scored three FA Cup goals in two games, taking his Everton total to sixty-three goals.

In this one season, Dean created two records that will probably never be broken in the top division; most league goals in a season, and most total goals for a season. He also created Everton club records that might never be broken; seven hattricks in a top flight season, a hattrick at Anfield, four goals in one game away at Burnley, and five goals in one game against Manchester United.

Along with the league and club records, Dean scored a goal against nineteen of the other twenty-one league clubs, and FA Cup goals against Preston North End and Arsenal. The two teams he failed to score against, West Ham United and Sunderland, luckily for them he only played against them once that season.

Ironically, in the game against West Ham United that Dean didn't play in because he was international duty, on 22nd October, Everton won 7-0. Dean's England, on the other hand lost 2-0 to Ireland at Windsor Park, Belfast on the same day. Would Dean have found himself on the score sheet on that day Everton beat West Ham 7-0 if he wasn't away on international duty? And what of the other game, away at Sunderland, were Everton won 2-0, whilst Dean was playing for England at Wembley in a famous 5-1 defeat against Scotland. Interesting thought.

To highlight, understand and illustrate what a goal machine Dean was this season, at the back of the book, there is a breakdown of the goals, the date they were scored, the team they were scored against and the number he scored in each of those games. It will dumbfound you.

The season is one never to be forgotten, but sometimes it is forgotten that Dean didn't achieve all these goals by himself. He needed the help from the rest of the team, and not just the crosses from Alec Troup from the left wing and Ted Critchley from the right wing, it was a real team effort. Something Dean was quick to point out.

But even more than that, he was aided by the Everton trainer, Harry Cooke. Without Cooke, Dean wouldn't have reached the sixty league goals, and Dean was always eternally grateful to Cooke, who he seen more as a father figure and great friend, much more than a trainer.

After pulling a thigh muscle in the penultimate game of the season against Burnley, Cooke stayed with Dean in his house and changed hot plasters and bandages every two hours for three nights on the run, in the hope Dean would be fit to face Arsenal. Dean has been quoted as saying, "Without him, I would never have played that day and never broken the record", and "I owe a good deal to that man. He nursed some of my injuries more successfully than the doctors."

Harry Cooke, was possibly the greatest Everton unsung hero.

When Dean finished the season with his sixty league goals he'd joined the other Everton legends that had also been the First Division's top league goal scorers; Jack Southworth (1893/94), Jack Settle (1901/02), Alex 'Sandy' Young (1906/07), Bert Freeman (1908/09), Bobby Parker (1914/15), and Wilf Chadwick (1923/24).

What a season, what a legend.

Three Hattricks in Eleven Days

Season 1928-29

After finishing the 1927-28 season with his 12th hattrick for Everton, Dean scored another on the opening day of the 1928-29 season, making it three consecutive games where he scored a hattrick, and thus creating another club record that as yet to be bettered. This time it was away to Bolton on 25th August, in a 3-2 victory that the Liverpool Courier put down to a, "magnificent performance was the direct outcome of highly scientific football applied with the maximum of speed and the minimum of effort."

It was an excellent way to open the season for the champions. The Daily Courier not only purred about the team performance but also of Dean, scoring one goal in the first half and two in the second half, "He obtained his three goals in excellent style, seizing his opportunities in a trice and applying the necessary touches."

Again, Dean didn't achieve these goals on his own, and was aided again by great passes and crosses from Weldon and Troup. It was the first of four hattricks that he would score before the end of the year.

Apart from another Dean hattrick, and another victory, the game was notable for the debut of Jimmy Dunn, one of Scotland's infamous "Wembley Wizards" team who beat England 5-1 at Wembley on 31st March 1928. Signed in April the previous season, Dunn would go on to be a great success at Everton, and a great friend of Dean's. As well as a practical joker off the field, Dean described Dunn as, "A very tricky ball player."

Dunn nearly scored on his home debut in the following game, a 0-0 draw with Sheffield Wednesday, when he hit the post with a 30-yard drive. As for Dean, Sheffield Wednesday man marked him out of the game. It was a clever tactic that worked for them again less than a week later in the reverse fixture, were they won 1-0.

In all fairness to Everton, Sheffield Wednesday would eventually win the league. Just beating Leicester City by a point. And they can thank their home record for their success. They won eighteen games, drew three and didn't lose a game. Away from home, they were poor, finishing the away table in 14th place, three below Everton.

In between the Sheffield Wednesday matches, Dean, with the help of Dunn, scored his second hattrick of the season, on 1st September, in a 4-0 win at home to Portsmouth. This hattrick came eleven months after Dean had inflicted another hattrick against Portsmouth, that time at Fratton Park.

It wasn't just Portsmouth who Dean enjoyed bagging hattricks against, on 22nd December, Dean grabbed his third hattrick against Newcastle United in a 5-2 victory at Goodison Park.

Sticking with the same team that didn't manage to score against Sheffield Wednesday, Everton beat Portsmouth comfortably. Dean's first two goals were both headers. His third goal, by the way the Daily Courier reported it, shows the skill that did exist back in the day, "Dunn, whom a section of the crowd have nicknamed "Tich," served up one of the finest passes of the game when he back heeled the ball through the backs for "Dixie" to almost break the net."

On the 8th September, Everton played their third game in eight days, away to Birmingham where Dean scored one goal in a 3-1 victory for Everton. According to the Daily Courier, he missed two good chances at the start of the game. They also reported he "received a blow on the leg."

A week later, Dean played again in a shocker at Goodison Park were Everton lost 6-2 to Manchester City, with five goals being scored by Tommy Johnson. By the end of the following season, Johnson would become a Toffee.

Dean then missed the next game against Huddersfield Town, because he was playing for the Football League against the Irish League at Winsor park, Belfast. He scored two goals in a 5-0 victory.

Back for the derby game at Goodison Park, Dean was man marked again, but the tactic allowed Dunn and Troup room to manoeuvre, and Troup scored the only goal of the game.

Following the derby game, Dean scored a hattrick in the Lancashire Senior Cup, in a 3-1 victory over Preston North End at Deepdale. Like a shark can smell blood, Dean was on the scent for goals, and scored seven in the next four games. Two of those goals were scored in the 2-1 Charity Shield win at Old Trafford over Blackburn Rovers.

Then through a mixture of being man-marked, carrying an injury, a little bit of bad luck, and the team not playing particularly well, the goals dried up somewhat. In six games between 27th October and 1st December, Everton scored three goals and conceded seven. The games were decided by a goal here and a goal there. Dean himself scored the only game at Goodison Park with a win over Bury.

Things improved, and Everton went on a six-game streak in which they won four and drew two. In amongst those set of results, Dean scored three hattricks in the space of eleven days. He even manged to score a goal against Leicester City, in a 3-1 win at Goodison Park, that the Daily Courier described as being as, "This type of goal from Dean is as good as a bottle of champagne."

The run of hattricks started on 22nd December against Newcastle, two years and two days after the last one against them. Dunn and Dean's partnership were mentioned as a factor in the 5-2 victory. The description of Everton's third goal in the Liverpool Football Echo certainly proved footballers at this time had skill and were entertaining, "Dean to Dunn, Dunn backheeled to Dean – result, a goal with a shot of unstoppable type."

After Newcastle opened the scoring in the third minute, Dean equalised in the fifteenth minute. The Liverpool Echo reported the goal to be a "grand slam" of a shot. Then thanks to a great goal from Martin, Everton were leading 2-1 at half-time. On 57 minutes, Dean extended Everton's lead, before Newcastle pulled one back. Two minutes later, in the 76th minute, Ritchie scored another for Everton, before Dean rounded things off with a goal seven minutes from the end.

Seven days later, Dean scored his second hattrick over the festive period, this time against Bolton Wanderers, bagging all three goals in a 3-0 win at Goodison Park. Surprisingly, sandwiched in between these two hattricks, Everton drew 0-0 with Sunderland at Goodison Park. The Daily Courier reported that it was an entertaining game and that Dean was always, "shadowed by four men."

The hattrick against Bolton was the debut of Jimmy Stein, and it was Stein who created the first and third goals for Dean. The first goal was a header and scored in a first half dominated by the visitors. In the second half, it was Everton's turn to dominate proceedings, with Dean completing his hattrick in the 75th minute. According to the Daily Courier's report, Dean's second was something to admire, "The second was the prettiest, for Dean, and Dunn worked their way right through the defence by judicious inter-passing before Dean almost ripped the meshes of the net."

Once again, the description of the goal shows football back in the twenties and thirties was as skilful as it is today. What a shame, all we have is grainy footage from the odd game.

Signing off the year with a hattrick in a 3-0 victory was a good way to end the year for Dean, and he didn't wait long to find his next hattrick. On the 1st January, at Goodison Park,

Everton beat Derby County in a 4-0, with all four goals coming in the first half. This was Dean's fifth hattrick of the season.

Dean was helped with the first goal, not from a clever pass from an Everton player, but from a Derby defender kicking fresh air, allowing Dean to score an easy goal after eleven minutes. Dean then hit the post before scoring a header, and a further goal in the final four minutes of the first half. In between Dean's first and second goal, Dunn scored one for himself and hit the crossbar in the second half.

Dean's hattrick made it three hattricks in eleven days. Surely another club record that will stand the test of time?

After starting the new year on fire, Everton then went five games without winning one. Just like earlier in the season the goals dried up. They scored one goal in those five defeats.

In the final game of those run of defeats, a 3-0 defeat against Huddersfield Town at Goodison Park, on 2nd February, Dean suffered a leg injury which kept him out for two matches.

Surprisingly, and not for the first time, Everton won both games in Dean's absence. A 2-1 against Liverpool at Anfield and a 5-2 victory over Blackburn at Goodison Park. Even more bizarrely, Blackburn's Roxburgh scored two own goals.

Dean returned with the opening goal in a 3-1 defeat away against Leeds United, before missing five games through not being fully fit. He did play a couple of reserve games and scored a couple of goals. The Daily Courier suggested he wasn't getting in the first team because he was suffering from rheumatism.

When he did return to the first team, he scored both goals in a 2-1 win away at Bury. But it would be his last goals for the season.

It was stop-start end to the season for Dean, playing only five times in the final fifteen games of the season, scoring three goals. Up until the injury against Huddersfield, Dean had scored 25 goals in 26 games. His total for the season was a remarkable 28 goals in 31 games.

It was an up and down season for both Dean and Everton. They went top of the league after three games, dropping down to thirteenth on the 1st December, climbed back up to eight in February, and then finished the season disappointingly in eighteenth position. Their end to the season was abysmal. They won one game in the last ten games, drawing one and losing eight. They lost the last six games of the season. Three of those last six games, Leicester City away, and West Ham and Manchester United all put four goals past them. They lost their last four home games of the season. Their away record was better than their home record. They literally nose-dived with eight games remaining.

There was some joy though, when they won the Charity Shield on 24th October, by beating Blackburn Rovers 2-1 at Old Trafford. And they did the double over Liverpool, a 1-0 win at home and a 2-1 win away. But overall, it was a disappointing season for the champions.

The end of the campaign was a warning, there was worse to come.

Going Down

Season 1929-30

Before the season started, Dean looked like he was back to full fitness, and in a practice match he scored six goals, with four scored in the first twenty minutes. Unfortunately, Everton had a couple of injuries to three of their regular first team players; including Troup, Virr and Griffiths.

Reasons to feel that Dean was back to his best increased on the opening game of the season, when it took him eleven minutes to open his account, with an equalising goal against FA Cup holders Bolton Wanderers at Goodison Park on 31st August. He scored a second goal on twenty-three minutes with his head, in an entertaining 3-3 draw. Everton were a little unlucky not to get all the points, as Bolton scored in the dying seconds to get a draw.

Two days later, Dean missed the second game of the season, away to Burnley, through injury. A Jimmy Stein goal, had Everton winning the game, but the same bad fortune in the first game was to repeat itself in similar fashion when Burnley equalised with seconds to go. The game ended 1-1. What was worse, the Everton goalkeeper, Arthur Davies was fouled and bundled into the back of the net for the goal. There was further suspicion that one of the Burnley players put ball into the net with his hands.

Dean was back for the third game of the season, just five days after the Burnley game, which happened to be the Merseyside derby at Anfield. He scored two goals before half time. The first in the 16th minute, hooking a ball over his head and into the Liverpool net, and a second in the 41st minute after the goalkeeper fumbled the ball in front of Dean. Everton beat

Liverpool comfortably 3-0, with Martin getting Everton's other goal.

After the derby game, Everton won one game in the next six matches. They drew two and lost three games on the bounce. Dean kept up his record of scoring in every game in his first eight games. A total of twelve goals in his first eight games. Scoring in every game would continue for Dean, and in the first twelve games of the season, he scored sixteen goals in total.

The only game Everton won from that run of six games after the derby victory, came away at Portsmouth on 28th September, in a 4-1 win, with Dean grabbing three goals. It was the third hattrick he'd scored against Portsmouth, with his last one coming just over a year ago at Goodison Park.

Portsmouth deservedly took the lead in the sweltering heat in the 22nd minute of a first half where they battered Everton but still somehow finished the half 2-1 down. The weather was so hot that a spectator died in the first half from the heat and a bandsman also collapsed.

One minute after Portsmouth had took the lead, Jimmy Stein equalised for Everton. Later in the half O'Donnell sent an inch perfect cross for Dean, who scored one of his trademark back-headers.

Dean's second goal is a bone of contention to my uncle, who was told by his grandad who was at the game, that in this game Dean scored a hattrick of headers. The report in both the Liverpool Football Echo and the Daily Courier are certain Dean's first and third where headers but the second goal is vague in their description of the goal. The build-up is clear, with Ritchie and Dean inter-passing, and from Ritchie's cross, Dean goes up with the Portsmouth goalkeeper Gilfillan, and according to the Daily Courier, "Dean pipping the goalkeeper on the post, hitting the ball towards the goal and then leaping over Gilfillan's prostrate body and following the ball into the net."

The Liverpool Football Echo described a similar moment up to Ritchie's cross then, "the ball going at an angle that led Gilfillan to dive the wrong way, so that Dean was able to slip over the goalkeeper's fallen body and turn the ball into the net."

Was it a header or did the "turn the ball into the empty net" or "following the ball into the net" mean that Dean finished the goal off with foot and a tap in?

Unfortunately, with no video replay and the vagueness of the description, who knows.

However, Dean's third goal was definitely a header and he scored it in the 80th minute of the game. But it came about through an unexpected way, as described by the Daily Courier, "he tried to kick the ball home, but misfired and the ball bounced straight up to his forehead."

Bizarre. But they all count. And whether this game was Dean's first hattrick of headers for Everton or not, it was still another hattrick to add to the collection. Dean also hit the bar with a header, as well as Richie missing an open goal.

One game later, away to Sunderland in a 2-2 draw, Dean got an ankle injury that kept him out for the next two games. Missing a 1-1 draw with Arsenal at Goodison Park, and a 5-2 defeat away at Aston Villa.

He returned on 19th October, for the visit of Middlesbrough, and scored one of the goals in a 3-2 victory. He scored a goal in each of the next three games against Blackburn Rovers, Newcastle United and West Ham United, before limping off five minutes from the end of a 2-0 defeat at Goodison against Huddersfield Town.

The injury was a bad one, and required an operation to remove "a foreign body" from his ankle, a splinter of bone. The injury kept him out for the following five matches. He came back for the Christmas Day fixture at home to eventual champions for the second year running, Sheffield Wednesday. But a hefty challenge on his other ankle kept him out of action for the next two games.

In the seven matches Dean missed, Everton had slumped to one place off the bottom of the league, and had taken some heavy defeats. In his absence they'd won one, drew two and lost five, conceding sixteen goals along the way, and scoring just seven goals. Four of the goals came in one match where they even lost that, 5-4 to Leicester City at Goodison Park.

After seventeen minutes of the game against Leicester, Everton were winning 2-0. But somehow, just after the 47th minute, they were losing 5-2. They clawed a couple of goals back but it was to no avail, it was another defeat without Dean.

In another match, a 0-0 draw away at Birmingham City, Everton cursed Lady Luck again, as they were convinced that they had scored a goal, after the Birmingham goalkeeper had apparently dragged the ball over the line from a shot by Wilkinson, but the referee didn't give it. Things just weren't going for them.

This continued on Dean's return, a home game against Liverpool. Dean scored two, as Everton were leading 3-1, but threw away the points again, with the final score being a 3-3 draw.

Dean followed the two goals against Liverpool with two each in the next two games. A 4-2 victory in the FA Cup away against Carlisle United, and a 4-0 home win against Derby County. But his ankle injury came back to give him trouble in a 2-1 victory against Manchester City on 5th February.

He missed Everton's heavy 4-0 defeat away to Arsenal, before returning for another the next five games, in which he scored two goals.

But Dean had been carrying ankle injuries for too long and missed a 4-2 defeat at home to Birmingham, before completing just two more games before the end of the season.

His ankle injury was so bad, that it kept him out of action for the last five games of the season, where surprisingly Everton finished strongly, winning four and drawing one, and scoring fifteen goals in total. Tommy White even managed a hattrick of his own on the final game of the season, a 4-1 win against Sunderland.

From the first game of the season to the last, Lady Luck seemed to shun Everton. On the last game of the season, four other clubs could have been relegated, but they all won, and Everton were relegated for the first time in their history.

Only two points separated the bottom five teams, and only four points separated the bottom nine.

In the days when it was 2 points for a win, Everton may well have not been relegated if their opponents in the first 2 games of the season hadn't have scored last minute goals, or they held on to the 3-1 lead they had over Liverpool on 4th January.

Indeed, if Everton wouldn't have lost 1-0, away at Newcastle on 8th March, and just got a draw, it would have been Newcastle who would have been relegated. That's how unfortunate the season had been.

But it was Everton's home record, more than anything else that let them down. They had the worst home record in the division, with only six wins. Sheffield Wednesday, Aston Villa, Grimsby Town and Birmingham City all scored four goals and collected all the points at Goodison Park.

Away from home, they recorded the sixth best record in the division. However, some of the defeats were heavy. Aston Villa, Bolton Wanderers and Leicester all scored five goals against them. Sheffield Wednesday, Blackburn Rovers and Arsenal all put four past them.

Once again, it's notable that Dean was injured for most of the season. He played just 27 games in total, scoring a remarkable 25 goals, with 23 league goals from just 25 league games, including his one hattrick for the season, against Portsmouth.

With all the injuries he had this season, as well as the operations, he still managed to score more league goals than any other player, and finish the season as Everton's top goal scorer.

Smashing Records

Season 1930-31

If season 1929-30 had been a season of injuries for Dean, then he certainly made up for it in season 1930-31. He competed 42 matches of the 47 games Everton played. Even better, he was back to his best, scoring 39 league goals in 37 games, and 9 goals in 5 FA Cup matches.

Not only did Dean help the team back to the top flight after just one season, but he also would go on to score six hattricks, with four in the league and two in the FA Cup.

Everton may well have fallen out of the top division the previous season, but they didn't wait around too long to get back into it, and would start off the season on fire. Season 1930-31 would turn out to be another record-breaking season for the club.

Surprisingly, it wasn't Dean who started the season in rapid goal scoring fire, it was team mate Tommy White. Whereas Dean had scored four goals in his opening six matches, White scored eight in his first five games, and two on the opening game of the season, away at Plymouth Argyle in a 3-2 victory.

Tommy White was another Everton player who stood in Dean's shadow, along with so many other Everton players of this era. In many ways, he was a bit of an unsung hero. This wasn't Dean's fault, Dean was just the focal point of the team for over a decade, grabbing the headlines and plaudits along the way for his natural goalscoring abilities and record-breaking statistics. But White, along with so many others played their part in Everton and Dean's success.

Bought from Southport in 1927, White was incredibly versatile and could play in several different positions, often used as striker and then as a centre-half. He scored two goals on his Everton debut in Dean's absence on international duty, in the 7-0 win over West Ham United in season 1927/28. It was the only game he played for the first team that season.

He would become Everton's leading goal scorer in season 1933/34, scoring 14 goals in 28 games. However, it should be noted that because of injury, Dean only played 12 league games that season, and still managed to score 9 goals.

But White was an excellent servant for Everton, playing a total of 204 games, and scoring 66 goals, all in the league. He also played at centre-half in the 1933 FA Cup final, becoming Everton's first Number 5.

White also scored three hattricks for Everton. His first hattrick was against Sunderland in the final game of season 1929/30, and the other two hattricks were scored against Portsmouth at Fratton Park in the second game of season 1931/32, in a 3-0 win, and against Blackburn Rovers at Goodison on 14th October 1933, in a 7-1 win.

By the end of this season, White would tally 10 goals in 10 games.

This was such an incredible year for Everton goal scorers that along with Dean and White, another four players scored ten league goals or more. Tommy Johnson and Jimmy Dunn scored 14 league goals each, Ted Critchley scored 13 and Jimmy Stein scored 10 league goals.

Everton won the first five games of the season, and Dean recorded his first goals of the season in his third match, in a 5-1 home win against Swansea Town. In the sixth game of the season, Everton drew 1-1 at home to Cardiff, with Dean getting Everton's goal, but he also picked up an injury which kept him out of two games. The first game he missed was Everton's first defeat of the season, a 3-2 defeat at home to Port Vale.

When he returned to the side, he would not miss the next thirty games. During that time, he would score forty goals in total, including six hattricks. His return game was against Charlton Athletic and he scored two goals, along with Dunn and Critchley in a 7-1 win at Goodison Park.

Dean's first hattrick of the season came on 22nd November at home against Stoke City in an easy 5-0 victory. He scored 2 goals in the first half, opening the scoring after 8 minutes, and he scored his second on 31 minutes, just two minutes after Tommy Johnson had increased Everton's lead. His third goal came in the 67th minute and Johnson scored his second on 73 minutes. The Liverpool Post and Mercury reported Dean's performance as a, "wholly satisfying display."

Dunn's performance was also highlighted, "His footwork was excellent and the openings he created offered fine opportunities for Dean."

Dunn's performance was so good that the Evening Express decided to use the pun, "Well Dunn Everton!"

They also pointed out that, "Dunn's was the mastermind that kept the Everton machine running so sweetly."

Dunn was to receive more plaudits from the same newspaper in the next game, when Everton lost 4-1 away to Bradford. Dean on the other hand, was reported as being "off form."

Dean's form must have returned for the next home game, on 6th December, when he went one better than he did in the Stoke game, by scoring four goals in a 6-4 win against Oldham Athletic. This was a game in which Everton were a goal behind on three occasions, and Dean scored the three equalisers.

His first equaliser came in the 6th minute, linking up with Stein, Dean "slammed" in a goal, just three minutes after Oldham had taken the lead. His second equaliser came on 40 minutes, and was described by the Liverpool Football Echo as a "long shot."

At half-time the game was level at 2-2, but within five minutes of the restart Oldham scored again. Four minutes later,

Dean scored his third equaliser of the game and with great skill. After a pass from Critchley, Dean coaxed the Oldham goalkeeper from his line and then placed the ball into the net.

Then Dean nudged Everton ahead in the 72nd minute with a header from a cross by Stein. Critchley pushed Everton further ahead before Oldham scored a fourth. Dunn finished off the scoring for the day with Everton's sixth of the day with one-minute remaining.

In the following game, away at Burnley, Everton conceded five in a 5-2 defeat. Dean and Stein got Everton's goals.

Dean then scored two headers and helped Everton overcome Southampton in their next home game in 2-1 win on 20th December. He then got one of the goals in a 2-2 draw away against Bury.

Then Dean scored four goals in the next home game, in a 9-1 hammering of Plymouth Argyle on 27th December 1930. Amazingly Jimmy Stein also scored four goals, and Tommy Johnson got the other goal. The score line equalled Everton's best league win, when they beat Manchester City by the same score on 3rd September 1906, when Alex 'Sandy' Young also scored four goals.

This was only the second time Everton had played Plymouth. The first encounter being on the opening day of the season, when Tommy White scored 2 and George Martin scored 1 goal in a 3-2 victory at Fratton Park. They would go on to play Plymouth again, 2 weeks later in the FA Cup at Fratton Park, and beat them 2-0.

In the 9-1 victory, Dean scored two goals in the first five minutes. His first after one minute, and the second in the fifth minute. At half-time Everton were winning 4-0. In the second half, Dean scored two goals in two minutes, in the 69th and 71st minute of the game. One minute before Dean got his third, Stein scored his hattrick, before getting his fourth with three minutes of the game remaining.

Dean scored another four goals, four weeks later in the FA Cup, on 24th January. This was the third time he'd scored four goals in just over nine weeks. This time the goals came away at Selhurst Park, in a 6-0 victory over Crystal Palace. The result was sweet revenge for Everton after they'd been beaten by the same score by Crystal Palace at Goodison Park, nine years earlier on 7th January 1922.

Even though Dean was suffering with a heavy cold, in the build up to the game, Dean told the Evening Express that he wanted to score six goals himself to avenge the defeat from 1922.

On a blustery afternoon, Everton played with the wind in the first half and went into the interval a goal to the good, thanks to Dean. In the second half, facing the wind, they somehow managed to score five goals, with three for Dean. His third goal was classic Dean; headed in from a corner from Stein.

Dean, like everyone else, loved the FA Cup. It was the king of cup competitions for many a year. To win "the Cup" was a great achievement for any club, a real prestige.

Dean scored on his cup debut, in a 1-1 draw at home to Fulham on 9th January 1926, and would go onto score 28 goals in 32 games for Everton. The twenty-eight goals would become another club record for Dean, and one that might never be broken.

Graeme Sharp came within eight goals away from capturing Dean's FA Cup record, and had to play an extra twenty games to get there.

This isn't to take anything away from Graeme Sharp, who sits in second place to Dean in the all-time Everton goal scoring charts, this is just to illustrate Dean's goal scoring pedigree in the competition. Indeed, Graeme Sharp is without doubt an Everton legend, helping the club to win two league titles, a FA Cup, and a European Cup Winners Cup in the marvellous side of the mid-1980's.

Two weeks after Dean had scored the four goals against Crystal Palace, he scored another hattrick away from Goodison Park. This time it was Charlton Athletics turn, in a 7-0 thrashing on 7th February. Five different Everton players scored that day. In the two games against Charlton in season 1930-31, Everton had scored fourteen goals against them, and conceded one.

The hattrick against Charlton, came in a spell of fourteen games in league and cup, from 27th December to 7th March, where Everton won every one of them, and scored an incredible sixty-five goals. With Dean helping himself to twenty-four goals of the sixty-five.

No matter what way you looked at Dean's statistics, it was goal after goal after goal. From the 4th October 1930 to the 18th February 1931, Dean scored in every home game. A total of 21 goals in 11 games, with 16 goals in the league. From the 6th December to the 3rd January he played 7 games and scored 15 goals. From the 17th January to 28th February he played 9 games and scored 17 goals.

In the 7-0 defeat of Charlton Athletic, Everton were leading 6-0 at half time, with all six goals coming in a 25-minute period. What made this goal scoring incredible was the game was still 0-0 leading up to 20 minutes of the game gone. Stein opened the scoring on 20 minutes. Two minutes later, after receiving a pass from Dunn, Dean scored. Both goals were hit with such a fury that the ball hit the net and came back on to the field.

Dunn, Critchley and Johnson scored a goal each in the next fifteen minutes, before Dean scored Everton's sixth in the 44th minute, after Critchley had seen a shot rebound off the woodwork. Dean completed his hattrick in the 87th minute after Gee sent him a perfect pass up field.

According to the match report in the Liverpool Post and Mercury, Dean could have scored more, Stein could have scored a hattrick himself, and the woodwork came to Charlton's rescue on more than one occasion. Furthermore, it seems that with six goals to the good at half time, and with a cup game against Grimsby Town to follow in the next game, Everton took their foot off the gas in the second half.

Everton beat First Division Grimsby Town 5-3 at Goodison Park in Round 5 of the FA Cup, just 10 months after Grimsby beat them 4-2 on the same ground, and helping relegate Everton. The win over Grimsby put Everton into the Quarter Final where they would play Southport.

Before the Southport game, Dean scored two goals against Barnsley in a 5-2 victory, and Everton also beat Nottingham Forest 2-0.

The Southport game, on 28th February was almost called off on the morning of the game because the snow was so bad in and around the ground. The game went ahead, and Everton went on to smash Southport 9-1, with Dean scoring another four goals in a game. He scored his first three goals within 35 minutes. At half-time, Everton led 7-0, with Critchley and Dunn scoring two each. Dean's goals came in the 4th minute, 30th minute, and 35th minute. He added a 4th goal in the 62nd minute.

It was Dean's final hattrick of the season, a total of six, and the 4th time he'd scored four goals in a game in a season. Four goals scored four times in a season by an Everton player, is yet another club record that will probably never be beaten.

Dean's 9 FA Cup goals in a season, also beat the club record set by Tommy Browell in season 1911/12, when he scored 7 goals in 5 games. The nine goals in the FA Cup in one season, is probably another record that will never been broken. Jackie Coulter in season 1934/35, Derek Temple in season 1965/66, and Graeme Sharp in season 1987/88, all scored six goals. All still one goal shy of Tommy Browell's total, and three goals shy of Dean's record.

Season 1930-31 was a success, and Everton were on fire. They scored in all but 3 of the 47 games they played, and amounted 121 league goals. They won 28 of the 42 league matches, and had the best home and away record of any team in the division.

At home they scored a goal in every game, won 18, drew 1 and lost 2, amassing 37 points from the 42 available, and scored 76 goals in the process.

Apart from the narrow 1-0 defeat in the semi-final of the FA Cup at Old Trafford, to eventual winners West Bromwich Albion, and the 1-0 defeat to Tottenham Hotspur and 2-0 defeat to Stoke City, Everton scored a goal in every away game they played.

They even beat every team in the league at least once.

The defeat in the FA Cup to West Bromwich Albion came after Everton had beaten them twice that season, both games finishing 2-1, with Dean scoring a goal in each game. West Bromwich Albion had great success themselves, winning the FA Cup and coming Runner's Up to Everton in the league.

Everton went top of the division in only their fifth game of the season, on 13th September and stayed there for the rest of the season, only being knocked off the top spot twice in that time, in mid-September and mid-October.

Having been in top spot for such a long time, Everton were now back on the march to the First Division with their sights on the top spot of the First Division.

Champions Again

Season 1931-32

Not many people would have believed that Everton, who had just won promotion from the Second Division after one season outside the top flight, would go on to win season 1931/32, the way they did. Boasting the best home record of the division and the second-best away record of the division. But that didn't tell half the story.

By the end of the season, the same team that created club records the previous season, would create even more club records, that to this day have never been matched or beaten. As for Dean, he would destroy the club record of hattricks scored by one player in one season, creating a new club record that will surely stand for ever. Dean would also set a milestone of league goals in a season that even he only beat once, in that great season of 1927/28 with his 60 league goals.

Before season 1931/32 started, Dean was given the honour of becoming the club's captain for the season. He had done the role previously on a number of occasions, but this was the first time it was his for keeps. It gave him great pride being the sheriff of Goodison, and the fearless Jock Thomson became his deputy.

Jock Thomson had signed from Dundee in March 1930, just weeks after Alec Troup had gone the other way. Although he was blameless for Everton's relegation only a few months later, he only played nine games, he was instrumental in their instant return to the top flight, missing just one league game all season. He was also a big part of the success that was to follow in the next two seasons. He would go on to play for the club for ten seasons, winning the First Division twice, the FA Cup and the Second Division. When his playing days were over, he went into management, managing Manchester City for a couple of seasons before retiring from the game altogether. He was a great deputy for Dean.

Something else to note before the season kicked off, was the Goodison turf, as reported in the Liverpool Echo, "The ground was billiard table-like, and football on it should be a joy after the experience of last year's mud-flats."

The season began with three wins, and two hattricks. Remarkably, neither hattrick was scored by Dean. The first hattrick came at Goodison on 29th August against Birmingham City in a 3-2 win, and was scored by Jimmy Dunn. Not that Dean didn't play his part, he laid on the second and third goals for Dunn to score.

Dean missed the second game of the season with an ankle injury sustained in the Birmingham win. Up stepped Tommy White, to score all three goals in a 3-0 win away at Portsmouth on 2nd September.

Dean was back in the team for the following game, but drew blanks in his next three games, with Everton winning one and losing the other two. When his first goal of the season came, he couldn't have chosen a better place to do it, and at the same time break another record.

It wasn't that Dean waited until the Merseyside derby at Anfield on 19th September before banging in his first goals of the season, and a 21-minute hattrick to boot, in a 3-1 victory over Liverpool, it was just one of those quirky things that happen in football.

The meeting was the 61st between Everton and Liverpool, and Dean's three goals brought Everton's goal tally against the reds to one hundred. The first goal came in the very first minute of the game, and Stein almost made it two a minute later. Then Liverpool equalised a minute after that, from a goal that looked offside to most but not the officials. It was all fast-flowing football. Then Dunn hit the crossbar, before Dean made it 2-1 on fifteen minutes. Six minutes later his hattrick was completed.

In scoring his eleventh league goal against Liverpool, Dean overtook Everton legend Alex 'Sandy' Young's league goals record in Merseyside derbies. He also beat Bobby Parker's lone hattrick in a 5-0 thrashing of Liverpool at Anfield, on 3rd October 1914, to create another record, as the only Everton player to score two hattricks at Anfield against Liverpool. And finally, he set a derby record no other Everton player as ever matched.

It didn't stop there, there was more to come in the following seasons.

It's another record that Dean has to his name, and for local pride sake, a record that every Evertonian can only hope one day gets beaten by another Everton player, or two.

Three weeks later, Dean got his second hattrick of the season, away at Sheffield United in a 5-1 victory, in a game Everton dominated so much that the Liverpool Post and Mercury reported, "if White had been in his customary form in front of goal they could have been a sensational margin – double figures at least."

Dean's first goal was a header in the first half, and his second and third goals had the Evening Express reporter in raptures, "Dixie Dean, the Everton centre-forward gave a dazzling display… he was the vital force in the Blues attack the methodical and virile leader of a football machine that worked with clocklike precision… His three goals were masterly efforts… Dean was irresistible. His shrewd side touches with head or foot, his leadership, and finishing was anything he has ever accomplished."

While the Liverpool Echo reported, "His solo drive was a thing to see to remember."

The following week Everton faced Sheffield Wednesday, a team who were also fighting for the top spot in the league and would finish third at the end of the season. It's easy to forget that during seasons 1928-29 to 1934-35, Sheffield Wednesday won the league twice and finished third on four occasions. Before dropping out of the division in season 1936-37.

Just as Dean had done to Sheffield United, he did to Sheffield Wednesday, and destroyed them, this time in a 9-3 victory at a patchy foggy Goodison Park, on 17th October, in a game Dean scored 5 goals, again.

Dean laid on the first goal for Jimmy Stein in the 22nd minute with another back-header, before scoring his first goal twenty minutes later in the 42nd minute from a two-man move with White. In a game that would end up 9-3, it was only 2-1 at half-time.

Dean scored his second of the game in an avalanche of goals in the second half, four minutes after the restart. Twenty-six minutes later he'd scored another three goals, with the goals coming in the 55th, 73rd and 75th minute.

The Evening Express gleefully told its readers that the result was the worst defeat Sheffield Wednesday had suffered since 1912, the time Aston Villa battered them 10-0.

The Evening Express was also certain that Dean had never been in greater form, "Dean was certainly at his best, and I say emphatically that not even during his 60 goals season did he play better."

It was also reported that Dean was now scoring 1.2 goals per game.

This was the third time in less than 10 months that Everton had scored nine goals against a team in a match. In the next game at Goodison on 31st October, they scored eight against Newcastle United.

As for the five goals Dean scored against Sheffield Wednesday, it was yet another little record he created; most goals by an Everton player to score in one game against Sheffield Wednesday.

After beating Aston Villa 3-2 away in the following game, Everton then battered Newcastle United 8-1 at Goodison Park, with Dean scoring two goals, along with Johnson and White. They were six goals to the good at half-time, and Dean was yet to get on the scoresheet. In total five different Everton players scored that game. The Evening Express called Everton's run, "phenomenal."

With the 3-2 victory over Aston Villa, Everton went to the top of the league, and stayed there for the rest of the season.

Dean missed Everton's next game, a 0-0 draw against Huddersfield Town because he was on international duty. But on his return, he would record another little record by scoring another five goals against one team. This time it was Chelsea, in another goal bonanza at Goodison, this time a 7-2 victory on 14th November. But what made this more incredible than the Sheffield Wednesday goals, from the five goals, four were scored with headers.

More astounding, his first three headers were all scored within ten minutes of each other. And to top that, all five goals were scored in 28 minutes. The five goals, the 28 minutes it took to score them, along with the four headers, with three in ten minutes, is surely another four club records that will never be matched or beaten by an Everton player for as long as the game exists.

And it's worth highlighting; **4 headers in a game, 3 inside 10 minutes**

The first header came from a Stein cross in the 5th minute. The second goal, in the 8th minute was described by the Liverpool Echo as a, "brilliant header, even more brilliant than the first goal."

When the third goal went in on the 15th minute, the Liverpool Echo suggested that there was, "pandemonium around the ground, and it was not surprising, for such brilliant ball control, especially with the head, was uncommon."

Dean scored a tap in the 24th minute, for his fourth goal, and his fourth header of the game came in the 33rd minute. In four games he'd scored fifteen goals. Another record that will never be beaten? More than likely.

Along with the scalps of Sheffield Wednesday and Manchester United, this was the third time Dean had scored five goals in a game against one team for Everton. Without sounding like a broken record, this was another little club record Dean set at Everton.

Two weeks later at Goodison, Dean scored another hattrick, and four goals in total, against Leicester City in another game were Everton scored nine goals in a game. This was their fourth time in less than a year they'd achieved this feat. It was also their 62nd goal of the season in 17 games. A set of results that is fair to say will never be beaten by another Everton team.

This time Dean scored one header in the 9-2 victory on 28th November. The header was his first goal of the match in the 6th minute, and he followed that up with Everton's 4th goal on 29 minutes. His third and fourth goal were spaced out in the 56 minute and 78th minute. Tommy White and Tommy Johnson also bagged two more goals each.

Four weeks later, Dean scored another hattrick, as Blackburn Rovers were beaten 5-0 at Goodison Park on Boxing Day. It was a case of revenge for Everton because the day before the game Everton lost 5-3 in the reverse fixture, with Dean scoring one of the goals, and gaining a penalty after being fouled by the Blackburn goalkeeper. It was a match that contained four penalties, of which Tommy White scored two for Everton.

In the Boxing Day game, Dean scored his first two goals in the opening ten minutes of the match, in the 4th and 7th minute, before adding a the third in the 46th minute.

It must have been a great time to follow Everton at home for the first half of season 1931/32. Apart from losing 1-0 against Manchester City on 12th September, Everton won all the other 9 games, and scored 49 goals. They put 9 goals past Sheffield Wednesday and Leicester City, 8 past Newcastle United, 7 past Chelsea, 5 past Blackburn Rovers and Middlesbrough, 3 against Birmingham City and Blackpool, and 2 against Derby County. An opening first half to a season, stuffed with so many goals that Evertonian's will be lucky to see ever again.

The hattrick against Blackburn was Dean's, sixth of the season. He'd now scored six hattricks between the 19th September to 26th December. It was his tenth hattrick in the last year. A truly incredible statistic that once again, is unlikely to be matched or broken by an Everton player.

Before the season ended there was still enough time for Dean to score two more hattricks, both at Goodison Park. Taking his tally to eight hattricks for the season. Another record never bettered by an Everton player. He had scored more hattricks in this one season than any other Everton player ever scored with the club.

The first of the two hattricks took place on 19th March in a 4-1 win against Huddersfield Town. In the run up to the game, Everton were in fine form and had won the previous 3 matches, 5-1 at home against Sheffield United, 3-1 away against Sheffield Wednesday, and 4-2 at home against Aston Villa.

Huddersfield were having a decent season, and would eventually finish 4th in the league. Dean had missed the reverse fixture in November due to international duties, but needed only 5 minutes to get the goal scoring underway. Dean's second goal of the game, in the 10th minute, was Everton's 100th league goal of the season. He rounded off the hattrick in in typical fashion with a back header in the 60th minute.

The final hattrick of the season came against West Ham United in a 6-1 spanking on 16th April. The win broke the club record, at that time, of consecutive games without defeat, ten in total. It was an easy win for Everton against a team who would eventually be relegated, and sweet revenge for the 4-2 defeat earlier in the season at Upton Park.

Dean opened the scoring after 4 minutes, and scored two in the second half, in the 66th minute and the 75th minute. He even found time to hit the crossbar, in yet another game he could have scored more than the three goals he did.

Two games after the 6-1 hammering of West Ham United, Everton won the league at Goodison with a 1-0 win against Bolton Wanderers. The scorer of the goal, one William Ralph 'Dixie' Dean, and a goal from another header.

What a fantastic season of goals and triumph. Eulogies came from far and wide and were printed in the Liverpool Echo. Herbert Chapman of Arsenal was quoted as saying that the Everton team, "always play football of the best type. They are a pleasure to meet both on and off the field of an example of all what is best in the game."

Willie Maley, the Celtic manager and Celtic legend, stated, "I wish the Everton management continued success in our national game, to which they have added deeds of the highest merit."

The Derby County chairman said of the Everton team, "they have played most attractive and finished football, thrustful and determined, and above all clean and sportsman like."

Middlesbrough manager, Peter McWilliam was quoted as saying, "Clean, scientific football, as played by Everton deserves success."

Other eulogies appeared, and in a time when the city of Liverpool was still in the county of Lancashire, other Lancashire clubs thanked Everton for bringing the championship home to Lancashire, most notably Manchester City and Blackburn Rovers.

Winning the First Division the season after gaining promotion from the Second Division as champions isn't an easy achievement, so hat's off to the Everton team of 1931/32.

Case in point, before the start of season 2019/20, only 5 clubs have ever done it; Liverpool (1905/06), Everton (1932/32), Tottenham Hotspur (1950/51), Ipswich (1961/62) and Nottingham Forest (1978/79).

Everton's home form was superb and record-breaking. To date, they have never bettered the amount of winning games at home in the top flight; winning eighteen games from twenty-one. And they've never scored as many goals at home as they did in season 1931/32, scoring 84 league goals. The winning teams of seasons 1939 and 1970 were one win away with seventeen victories, and as for the most goals from any Everton team in the top flight, the nearest was both the teams in season 1927/28 and 1938/39, who both scored twenty-four goals less than the team in season 1931/32.

The only time an Everton team got near to the 84 goals scored in season 1932/33, came from the team that won promotion the previous season with 76 goals. They also recorded 18 home wins and drew 1 more game. However, that wasn't in the top flight.

For the second year running, Dean did what most top goal scorers never achieve, in that he scored more goals than the number of games he played. This was the third time he'd achieved such a feat in the last five seasons. On this occasion it was 46 goals in a total in 39 games, with 45 goals coming in the league in 38 games, and 1 goal in 1 game in the FA Cup.

On the hattrick front, the eight he scored in one season, is fair to say, will never be beaten by an Everton player. Dixie Dean was truly a goal machine.

Up for the Cup

Season 1932-33

Season 1932-33 completed a hattrick of successes for Everton Football Club, in something that was described by Pathe News as "unparalleled in football history."

After winning promotion in blistering fashion in season 1930/31, then winning the top division the following season 1931/32, Everton won the FA Cup in season 1932-33. This was some achievement back in the 1930's. They even found time to win the Charity Shield. In the days when there was only league, FA Cup games, and the Charity Shield, there was no other glory left in English football, what else was there left to do?

It was another season without serious injury for Dean, missing just 3 league games, he played in 39 league games, scoring 24 goals. In total he scored 33 goals in 46 games for the season, but more importantly he scored one of the goals in the FA Cup final, a 3-0 victory over Manchester City.

The 1933 FA Cup final was different to any cup finals before it, because it was the first time that players wore numbers on the back of their shirts for identification. Everton wore numbers 1 to 11, and Manchester City wore numbers 12 to 22. Dean's number was number 9.

The final was different also because both teams naturally played in blue, and regulation rules stated that if team colours clashed then both teams had to wear alternative colours. Everton played in white shirts, black shorts, and black socks with a blue trim. Manchester City played in red shirts and socks and white shorts.

Dean scored Everton's second goal of the game in the 52nd minute, a header from a long cross from Cliff Britton. Earlier in the game, Dean was also involved in Everton's first goal, putting pressure on the Manchester City goalkeeper, who dropped the ball at the feet of Jimmy Stein, to score the opening goal in the 41st minute. The goal came 2 minutes after Dean had uncharacteristically missed a sitter from only three yards from goal. The third goal was scored by Jimmy Dunn from a corner kick in the 80th minute.

Dean's record in the FA Cup in season 1932/33 was excellent. He scored 5 goals in 6 games. Scoring a goal in every round except the 2-1 semi-final win against West Ham United.

The team that was part of the trilogy of successes for Everton between 1930 to 1933, was full of great footballers and one or two legends for the club. Example, goalkeeper Ted Sagar.

Sagar was the first Everton goalkeeper to wear the Number One jersey, and the only Everton player that didn't miss a single game in season 1932-33. After joining Everton as an apprentice in season 1929-30, Sagar would stay at the club until season 1952/53, keeping 120 clean sheets in 497 games, winning 2 league titles and the FA Cup. He is still the longest serving Everton player of all time, staying with the club for 24 years and 5 weeks. Creating a record that will probably never be broken.

Dean admired Sagar, and once said, "A team feels very secure when you have someone like Ted in goal. He was one of the greatest."

Along with Dean and Sagar that day was Cliff Britton, the first Everton player to wear the Number Four shirt, who Dean described as, "One of the finest half-backs in the history of the game."

Gordon Watson, went further, "they used to say that Cliff Britton was so talented, he would centre the ball so the lace faced away from Dixie."

Signed from Bristol Rovers in 1930, Britton would stay at Everton until the outbreak of the Second World War, playing 242 games, and playing once in the team that won the 1938/39 championship.

Britton would eventually move into management, helping Burnley gain promotion to the First Division and guiding them to the FA Cup final in season 1946/47. In 1948 he became the first ex-Everton player to manage Everton, taking over the reins from Theo Kelly. He managed Everton between the years 1948 to 1956, with mixed fortunes. Unfortunately, under his stewardship Everton were relegated on goal difference in season 1950/51. Three seasons later he helped them to promotion back to the top division, finishing second on goal difference to winners Leicester City. In February 1956 he was relieved of his Everton managerial duties.

The other two goal scorers in the 1933 FA Cup final, Jimmy Stein, who wore the Number Eleven shirt, and Jimmy Dunn who wore the Number Eight shirt, had excellent careers at Everton, both playing their part in the success of the early 1930's.

Both were signed from Scottish clubs and both played for Everton for 7 seasons. Stein signed from Dunfermline in April 1926, and Dunn from Hibernian in April 1928, after being part of the Scotland "Wembley Wizards" team of 1928.

Stein would go on to replace Alec Troup, the man who supplied Dean with so many goals. "I have to thank Alec as much if not more than anybody else for helping me to score goals", Dean said of Troup.

Stein played 217 games in total for Everton and scored 65 goals. Dunn played a total of 155 games for Everton and scored 49 goals.

The 1933 FA Cup team was full of excellent players, including the first Everton player to wear the Number 3 shirt, and the player who was known as "the Prince of Full Backs"; Warney Cresswell.

Dean joked that Cresswell was always the last to go to the bar for a round of drinks but was adamant that, "No better full-back ever played"

Bought from Sunderland in February 1927 for £7,000, Cresswell played for Everton until May 1936, playing 308 games in total, and winning 2 First Division titles, a Second Division title, the FA Cup and 2 Charity Shields.

Everton's first Number 6, Jock Thomson and Everton's first Number 2, Billy Cook, would both be at the club the next time Everton won the top division in season 1938/39. Like Cresswell, at Everton, Thomson would win 2 First Division titles, 1 Second Division title, a FA Cup and 2 Charity Shields. Signed from Dundee in March 1930, Thomson would play a total of 296 games, scoring 5 goals, and he would become Everton's captain when Dean departed the club.

As for Billy Cook, Dean described him as, "a storming full-back with a powerful kick." Cook would gone on to play 250 games at Everton and score 6 goals.

Everton's first Number Five was Tommy White, and according to Dean, White was "the most versatile footballer ever." White was signed from Southport in 1927, and played 1 game in the title winning season 1927/28. In that 1 game he scored 2 goals in Dean's absence on international duty, when Everton battered West Ham United at Goodison 7-0.

Also, in Dean's absence through injuries in season 1933/34, White would be Everton's top goal scorer with 14 goals in 28 league games. In the season Everton gained promotion from the Second Division, White scored 10 league goals in 10 games, and 18 goals in 23 games in the title winning team of season 1931/32. In total, he would go to play 204 games for Everton, scoring 66 goals.

Albert Geldard, Everton's first Number 7, replaced Ted Critchley for the final and supplied the cross for the third goal. Dean said Tommy Lawton once told him that Geldard was so fast that he could catch pigeons.

Like Tommy White, Geldard scored on his debut, this time in a 2-0 victory against Middlesbrough on 19th November 1932. In the following game, he scored again, in a 2-2 draw against Bolton Wanderers at Goodison. Geldard played 180 and scored 37 goals.

Everton's other player that day was Tommy Johnson, and he wore the Number Ten shirt. When Johnson signed for Everton from Manchester City in March 1930, the City fans were up in arms about the transfer because he was a great goal scorer for them. At Everton, Johnson would go on to play 161 games, and score 65 goals. A decent record in anyone's books.

Along with Ted Sagar, Johnson missed only 1 league game in the side that clinched the title in season 1931/32. In March 1934, nearing the end of his career, Johnson left Everton and joined Liverpool. He would play 36 league games and score 8 goals for Liverpool.

The FA Cup final team of 1933, was full of stars.

But if the FA Cup final was the highlight of the season for Dean, then the Charity Shield, played earlier in the season was a close second, and also part of his 37 Everton hattrick story.

On the 12th October, Everton played Newcastle United at St James' Park in a 5-3 thriller where Sagar saved a penalty, and Dean scored 4 goals, 3 with his head. In doing so he created another two little records that any future Everton player is doubtful to beat; scoring four goals in a Charity Shield match, and scoring three headers in a Charity Shield match.

The first header came in the 21st minute of the game from a cross by Stein. Stein also provided the cross for the second header in the 30th minute, and the third header came in the 88th minute of the game. Sandwiched between header two and three, Dean scored with his foot and the goal was described by the Liverpool Echo as, "a masterpiece of a goal."

In the league, Everton started with a defeat against West Bromwich Albion, followed by two wins against Sheffield Wednesday and Birmingham City. But the season was littered with inconsistency. They would win a couple, lose a couple, win one, lose one, draw one, etc. It was also a season that Dean was closely marked.

Dean's other hattrick came at Goodison Park against Leicester City in a 6-3 victory on 8th March. The game was the debut for the new Leicester goalkeeper Sandy McLaren, and he did what the Luton Town goalkeeper had to do only four days earlier at Goodison Park in the FA Cup; pick the ball out of the net six times. Everton won that tie 6-0, on their march to Wembley for the first time.

Against Leicester, Dean scored his first goal in the 16th minute with a trademark back header. The Liverpool Echo suggested the Leicester City goalkeeper had been, "baptised in the arts of the most famous centre forward the game has ever known."

Two more goals came in the second half, in a performance that was marvelled by the local press. "I think Dean's inspired game, a restlessly busy game, in which he showed more fire and enthusiasm than for months, was chiefly responsible for the victory" the Liverpool Echo enthused.

By the end of the season with the FA Cup in hand and the Charity Shield, Dean's two hattricks could have been more. On six other occasions Dean score two goals in a game, including home games against Manchester City, Wolves, and Sunderland, away games against Bolton Wanderers, and a home and away victory against Liverpool. Indeed, in the derby game at Goodison Park, Dean hit the crossbar and had several chances in the first half to score more goals. And the game against Bolton he had one shot saved and pushed on to the post.

When the final whistle was blown on the season, the reigning champions had enjoyed great cup success but had done little in the league, hovering mid-table for the entire season. At Goodison Park, Everton's record was better than eventual champions Arsenal, and the fourth best in the division. But away from home only Leicester City and the two teams relegated that season, Blackpool and Bolton Wanderers, had a worse record than Everton.

With Dean in the team, Everton were never a one-man team, but Dean was the focal point and not for the first time, Everton missed him when he wasn't available to play. In the three games Dean missed in the season, Everton lost all three, and scored one goal.

Broken Bones

Season 1933-34

Season 1933/34 was the only full season Dean had at Everton where he didn't score a hattrick for the first team. This wasn't surprising because he only managed to play twelve games all season, all in the league. He was plagued by injury. However, he still managed to score nine goals from those twelve games. This season, possibly more than any other season while Dean was at the club, Everton didn't have a replacement for Dean's goals or influence on the pitch, and they paid the price, struggling all season.

Dean and Everton started the season brightly with a 1-0 win at home to West Bromwich Albion. Dean scored in the 32nd minute with a header to open his account for the season. He also hit the underside of the crossbar later in the first half. It might have only been a 1-0 win but the Liverpool Post and Mercury was adamant, "Let it be put on record straight away that Everton won handsomely."

The following game, away at Derby County, Everton led after the 27th minute of the game thanks to Dean. Unfortunately, they couldn't hold on to the result and Derby equalised with two minutes remaining.

More frustration came in the following game, away at Birmingham City, when they squandered a 2-0 lead, both goals courtesy of Dean, and drew 2-2, when Birmingham equalised with fifteen minutes remaining. Everton couldn't have got off to a better start when Dean scored after 40 seconds. He grabbed his second in the 37th minute, but once again, they shot themselves in the foot. The opening goal was his 300th of his career in 311 matches.

Typical Everton were at it again in the fourth game of the season, this time at Goodison Park, when unbeaten they faced Sheffield Wednesday who had lost all three games of the season so far. Everton lost 3-2, with even more tragic-comic intervention. Already a goal down, Sheffield Wednesday scored their second in bizarre fashion. Described in the Evening Express, as a "lucky goal", a ball was lofted into the Everton area, and the goalkeeper Billy Coggins, a replacement for the injured Sagar, came racing out of his goal. His left leg collapsed underneath him, and as he fell to the ground the ball bounced in off his head and landed in the back of the net. You wouldn't know whether to laugh or cry. To make matters worse, Coggins didn't come out for the second half and Critchley ended up in goal.

Sheffield Wednesday scored a third before Everton, with fourteen minutes remaining, decided to do something about it. First, they got a penalty which White converted. Then four minutes later Dean scored a header from a corner by Geldard but it wasn't enough, they'd lost for the first time in the season.

With Sagar back in goal, Everton travelled to Manchester City, the team they had defeated in the cup final less than five months before. Geldard gave Everton the lead before City equalised. Dean then made it 2-1, but in the 67th minute, City got their second equaliser, and the game ended 2-2.

Dean was on the scoresheet again, his sixth game on the trot with a goal, when champions Arsenal came to Goodison Park on 23rd September. Everton started quickly and stayed focused throughout, and ran out 3-1 winners. After Dean scored the opening goal, he was pushed in the back in the penalty area, and White stepped up and scored. It was 2-0 at half-time, but Dean was carrying a leg injury. He came out for the second half but left the field after four minutes. Five minutes later, Dean was back on the pitch. Dean laid on the goal for Dunn to get Everton's third in the 76th minute. Everton continued to batter the Arsenal goal. With two minutes remaining Arsenal got a consolation goal.

It was a great victory against the champions, who would retain the title come the end of the season, but it came at a cost – Dean was injured.

Three days after the victory over Arsenal, the Evening Express ran an article stating Dean's injury occurred when he turned quickly and twisted his left ankle. After being examined by a specialist, two small pieces of bone in the ankle joint were the problem, and Dean had to have an operation to have them removed, keeping him out for a reported four weeks. It was a similar ankle problem to the one he had in November 1929, but this time it was the other ankle.

Scoring seven of Everton's eleven goals in the opening six games, Dean was going to be missed. And he was. Everton played six games in his absence, and scored eleven goals, which mightn't sound too bad, but seven of the goals were scored in one match, a 7-1 hammering of Blackburn Rovers. White scored a hattrick. The other five games they lost four and drew one. One of the games was a 3-0 defeat by Arsenal in the Charity Shield. In total Everton conceded thirteen goals.

Dean returned five weeks later on the 4th November against Huddersfield Town, but after 20 minutes he was injured in a collision with the Huddersfield goalkeeper Turner. Dean had to leave the field. Again, he returned with his leg bandaged up and limped his way to the end of the match. Everton lost 1-0.

Two days later, the Liverpool Echo reported that Dean had "cartilage trouble" and he would be fit in a day or two. Then all went quiet. They then reported on the 5th December that Dean was due to have the cartilage removed and would be out for a further two weeks. The Liverpool Post and Mercury reported the following day that Dean would have the cartilage in his knee removed.

In total, Dean missed eighteen games, including a 3-0 defeat by Tottenham Hotspur in the FA Cup.

He returned to the reserves in early February and scored the winning goal in a 2-1 victory over Bury at Goodison Park. Staying in the reserves, he scored the opening goal away at Newcastle United, in a 2-1 defeat.

But it wasn't until the 24th February, that he made his return to the first team in a 1-1 draw against Blackburn Rovers at Ewood Park.

Clearly still not 100% fit, Dean didn't play in the first team for the next seven games but played for the reserves, scoring 10 goals, including a hattrick.

He returned on the 21st April, and scored in a 1-1 draw with Portsmouth at Goodison Park, but was injured once more. He missed the next game against Huddersfield Town before playing in the two remaining games of the season, a 3-2 defeat away at Sunderland and a 2-2 draw at Goodison Park on the last game of the season, scoring one of the Everton's goals.

This season was a disappointing one for Dean and Everton. They finished 14th in the league and were knocked out of the FA Cup in the Third Round. Bizarrely, they beat the champions Arsenal home and away, two of only eight games that Arsenal lost in the league all season. And yet, they lost to Arsenal 3-0 in the Charity Shield at Goodison Park.

Apart from a 7-1 mauling of Blackburn Rovers, a 4-0 victory over Sheffield United, both at Goodison, and beating the champions Arsenal home and away, the season was one to forget. Not just for Dean and his injuries, but for the club too. Everton even managed to embarrass themselves by losing to Newcastle United 7-3 at Goodison Park on Boxing Day. Newcastle would eventually be relegated along with Sheffield United. Everton couldn't even muster an away win against any of the eight teams that finished below them in the league.

This was a long way away from the success of the last three seasons.

For Dean, this was the first time in eight seasons at Everton that he didn't end up as top goal scorer for the club. Tommy White finished the season top scorer with 14 goals in 30 games, with 28 of the games in the league. Dean scored 9 goals in only 12 games, not a bad return for a season decimated by serious injuries.

If it wasn't for the injuries, it's fair to say, things would have been different.

Back to the Top of the Pile

Season 1934-35

Recovered from two operations and other injuries from the previous season, Dean started season 1934/35 with a goal on the opening day of the season after just 34 seconds, against Tottenham Hotspur at White Hart Lane on 25th August. It was a header with the faintest of touches from Dean in a 1-1 draw.

In the second game, at Goodison Park against Leicester City, Dean scored the opening goal of the game on 25 minutes, in a 2-1 win for Everton. The other goal scorer was winger Charlie Leyfield. Leyfield also delivered the centre for the goal Dean scored. This was Leyfield's debut game. He was only on the pitch because Geldard was injured. What a start.

Leyfield would go on to play in the next nine games, scoring four goals, before Geldard returned to the first team. One of the goals he scored came against Preston North End at Goodison Park, scoring direct from a corner kick. An unusual occurrence this might have been, but the following season Stoke would score a goal direct from a corner against Everton too.

Geldard kept Leyfield out of the first team for the rest of the season, except for one game, in which Leyfield scored both goals in a 2-2 draw away against Manchester City.

It's hard to believe with the impact he had in the brief spell in the first team, 7 goals in 11 games, that he didn't become a regular, but it shows how hard it was to get in the first team and stay there, injury free.

Signed in December 1930, Leyfield was mainly a reserve player, and waited until the 29th August 1934 before he made his debut. The following season, with Stein and Coulter each still recovering from a broken leg, Leyfield started the first ten games of the season, scoring on the opening game of the season, before picking up an injury. He returned later in the season, but by then, Everton had already signed Torry Gillick, and Leyfield opportunities in the first team got less and less.

Used intermittingly in the first team for the following season, Leyfield took up an offer from Second Division Sheffield United. Later he joined Doncaster Rovers. His Everton career was short but an interesting one, finishing with 13 goals in 38 league games.

As for Dean, his injuries were clearly behind him, and his recovery was there for all to see. He didn't miss any of the first 36 games of the season, scoring 23 goals in the process, including a goal in the first four games of the season.

When Dean wasn't scoring, Coulter, Cunliffe and Stevenson all chipped in with goals. Between them, in ten games between 29th December to 16th February, they managed to score twenty-two goals. Coulter even scored a hattrick against Sunderland in a 6-4 victory, in the replay of Round Four in the FA Cup, at Goodison Park. Dean said that game was the greatest game he was ever involved in, and probably, "the greatest match ever played."

Dean didn't even score that day. What a game that must have been.

Along with Coulter's hattrick and a goal for Stevenson, Geldard was also on the score sheet. In the previous round of the cup, Geldard helped himself to a hattrick against Grimsby Town at Goodison Park in a 6-3 victory. Geldard pitched in with seven goals in that period of ten games.

But before Geldard and Coulter's hattricks, Dean showed them how to do it, on the 29th December at Goodison Park in a 5-2 victory over Tottenham Hotspur.

Everton had played Tottenham Hotspur four times in the calendar year and this was their first win. As well as the 1-1 draw on the opening day of the season, Everton had lost the other two games 3-0, once in the league and once in the FA Cup, both at White Hart Lane.

The victory was a crushing blow for Tottenham, and the score line didn't represent the game. According to the Liverpool Echo "five goals should have been eight or perhaps more."

Dean's first goal was a tap in the 12th minute, after the ball rebounded off the goalkeeper from a shot from Geldard. The second goal was scored in the 54th minute when he smashed it in from 15 yards. The hattrick was completed in the 64th minute from a header from a cross from Britton.

Dean had the chance to score a fourth, after being pushed in the back and earning a penalty, but decided to give Coulter the opportunity to score. Coulter missed. Not that it affected the outcome of the game.

The hattrick against Tottenham would be the only one Dean scored in the season. He came close on a couple of occasions. In three other games he scored a brace. Against Chelsea, Portsmouth, and Blackburn Rovers. The two goals he scored against Portsmouth on 10th November were described in the Liverpool Post and Mercury as, "the work of an artist."

He almost got another brace a week after the Portsmouth game, where he scored one goal against Stoke City, and had another disallowed for a push, in a 3-2 defeat.

When the season came to an end, Dean was top goal scorer at the club again, with 27 goals in 43 games, 26 goals came in the league from 38 games. After playing the first 36 games, he picked up an injury in the 4-4 draw against Leeds United at Goodison on the 6th March, in a game where Everton's Billy Cook had to leave the field after 25 minutes with a broken fibula, and a match that the Liverpool Post and Mercury described as "rugged".

Dean missed the following match, a 1-0 win away at West Bromwich Albion, and the following game, a 2-0 defeat against Arsenal at Goodison Park. Arsenal would go on to win the league for a third year running.

Dean then returned to play the next seven games, scoring four goals, before missing the final two games of the season, after being injured in a 4-1 defeat against Derby County.

As for Everton they finished the season 8th in the league. They may have finished higher but a run of just three wins in the final fifteen games of the season, including losing to Bolton Wanderers in the Quarter Final of the FA Cup, tainted the season. Their away record was also poor, the seventeenth best in the league.

At home, they had the third best record in the division, winning fourteen, drawing five and only losing two games, scoring 64 goals along the way. There were handsome wins, including scoring 6 goals against Grimsby Town and Sunderland in the FA Cup, and Sunderland again in the league. They also scored 5 goals against Tottenham Hotspur, Blackburn Rovers, Wolverhampton Wanderers and Stoke City. And they scored four goals against four other clubs; Preston North End, Huddersfield Town, West Bromwich Albion, and Leeds United. There was also Dean's single goal in a 1-0 victory over Liverpool at Goodison Park on 15th September, to boast about.

Away from home their form was awful, winning just two games, drawing seven and losing the other twelve. Bizarrely, the day after they beat Sunderland 6-2 at Goodison Park on Christmas Day, they lost the reverse fixture on Boxing Day 7-0.

If their away form, matched their home form, they would have won the league handsomely. Then again, Sheffield Wednesday and Sunderland could have said the same thing.

As for Dean, it was the ninth time in ten full seasons at Everton, he would finish top of the pile in the goal scoring charts.

Another Broken Toe

Season 1935-36

Just like the end of the previous season, Everton started the new season poorly, with just three wins in twelve games, and their away form was appalling. A hangover from the previous season.

And yet when the season began it offered great hope as they went to the top of the league after one game, with a cracking 4-0 victory over Derby County at Goodison on the 31st August. Dean did what he always seemed to do, score on the opening game of the season.

However, the away form was bad. They didn't score a goal in the first three away games, and didn't win one until late November. Along the way, there were some terrible defeats. Wolves beat them 4-0, and Liverpool and Middlesbrough both scored six past them.

It was during the Liverpool defeat, the third game of the season, that Dean broke a bone in his right toe which kept him out of the next seven matches. Three times he had to leave the pitch, starting in the 28th minute. He also struggled to return after the re-start, missing the first two minutes of the second half, and was withdrawn with fifteen minutes to go.

In his absence Everton won the following game 3-0 against Portsmouth. But that was the only win they could muster until Dean returned from the broken toe injury on 19th October. He scored one of the goals in a 5-1 victory against Chelsea.

Dean then played the next eight games, scoring one more goal, before being dropped for being out of form. The injuries by now were starting to show. In the one game he added to his tally, a 5-1 beating of Stoke City, Cunliffe scored four goals.

Dean missed the next five games. But typical of Dean, whilst playing for the reserves he scored a hattrick against Liverpool at Anfield, once more, in another 3-3 draw.

He returned again to the Everton first team on 22nd January with two goals in a 3-3 home draw against Bolton Wanderers. Although a great comeback game, the Evening Express reported, "Dean returned after the interval, but was limping. His left leg seemed to be troubling him."

He however stayed in the team for the next fifteen games, scoring eleven goals, before a groin injury forced him to miss the last away game of the season against Leeds United.

During the run of sixteen games, there was a spell where Dean was back to his goalscoring self, scoring nine goals in eight games, with a brace against Middlesbrough and Blackburn Rovers.

His performances in many of these games were singled out by the Liverpool Daily Post; "Dean led the Everton forward with skill, and the inside forwards should have had more goals had they been up to take the back passes which the captain put down for them." (the game against Middlesbrough).

"Dean gave the greatest heading, display I have seen for years, and he also used his feet, and Swift had to make a number of smart saves. Dean's display was grand." (the game against Manchester City).

"The work of Dean had been of best quality." (the game against Aston Villa).

Also, during this run of games, Everton came back from 3-0 down, away from home, to draw 3-3 with eventual champions Sunderland, with Dean scoring the equaliser in the 75th minute. The Evening Express reported, "Dean's touches were a joy."

The run of games came to an end with an injury away to Brentford on a slippery surface, with Dean then missing one game, a defeat away to Leeds United.

During the Brentford game, a bizarre incident happened where Dean, protesting against a foul the referee had given against him, was seemingly sent off by the referee. While he stood on the touchline, the referee ordered him to come back on!

Several days later the Liverpool Echo put this incident down to a "sporting gesture" by the referee.

This wasn't the first time such an incident had happened to Dean. Away on international duty, he went "shoulder to shoulder" with the Belgium goalkeeper, with the goalkeeper ending up in the back of the net. Dean was convinced there was no infringement and believed it was a fair goal. Moments later the England trainer came running on the pitch to tell him that he'd been suspended and sin binned for ten minutes.

Just another incident from a bygone era that you will never see again.

Dean returned, once more, for the penultimate home game of the season on 25th April, against Birmingham City. It was at this stage in the season he decided to score another hattrick. Everton were losing 3-2 at half-time, before they came back to claim a 4-3 victory. Not for the first time in his career, Dean scored all three goals with his head.

The first goal came from a corner kick from Leyfield, in the 9th minute, before Birmingham scored two goals in two minutes. Dean equalised in the 21st minute from another corner kick, this time by Gillick, and in the 50th minute Dean headed his third of the game.

The headed hattrick Dean scored against Birmingham City was another record he has set up for a future Everton player to try and beat. Along with the other two headed hattricks Dean scored for Everton, it is going to be some feat to equal or beat three hattricks by way of the head in an Everton career, because it is so rare to score three headed goals in a game. Duncan Ferguson, a modern-day 1990's master header of the ball tried his best, and once scored three headers in a 3-0 home win against Bolton Wanderers on 28th December season 1997-98. So, for someone to beat Dean's record is going to take some doing.

A further injury, sustained in the Birmingham game, this time a broken shoulder blade, eventually kept Dean out for the last game of the season, at home to Preston North End. It was a game anticipated to be the game Dean would break Steve Bloomer's goal scoring record. So much so that Bloomer was in the crowd that day to witness it for himself. Alas, Dean's injury kept him out of the side that went on to beat Preston North End 5-0. Everton got a penalty in the game too, so the chances of Dean being able to beat Bloomer's record was there for the taking, bar the injury. In his absence, Britton scored the spot kick.

When the season ended Dean had completed just 29 games, and scored 17 goals. It was a tough season all round for Dean and for Everton. They finished in 16th place in the league, and it was a true season of contrasting results and performances.

Everton's home record was average, finishing ninth best, but apart from eventual champions Sunderland, no one scored more goals at home than Everton. Everton racked up five goals against Chelsea, Stoke City, Middlesbrough, West Bromwich Albion and Preston North End. And they scored four goals against West Bromwich Albion, Sheffield Wednesday, Wolves, Blackburn Rovers, Grimsby Town and Birmingham City.

Their away record on the other hand was best described as appalling. They won just won game away from home, against Grimsby on 23rd November in a 4-0 victory. They didn't even beat relegated Aston Villa and Blackburn Rovers, drawing both games 1-1.

In Everton's defence, there were a couple of games where they were either unlucky or unable to see the game out, but over-all they were poor.

One of the games where they were unlucky not to win came against Stoke City on 4th April. Everton were leading 1-0, when Stoke were awarded a hotly disputed penalty by the referee when their player seemed to fall into the penalty area from outside the box, from an incident that many at the game didn't believe was a foul in the first place. The second Stoke goal came direct from a corner kick. This time the goal was reported to have been aided by the wind and a foul on the Everton goalkeeper.

On another occasion on 28th December, Everton were leading Derby County twice, 2-0 at half time and 3-2, in a thriller that ended all square at 3-3.

But these two games can't disguise the fact that away from home Everton just weren't good enough. They conceded more goals away from home than any other team in the division. Fifty-eight in total. Liverpool, Middlesbrough and West Bromwich Albion all scored six goals against Everton.

Dean's injuries couldn't have helped matters. In his absence Everton relied on Jimmy 'Nat' Cunliffe, one of the 1930's Everton players who is in some cases was another of those unsung heroes of that period, living in the shadow, like so many others, of Dean and then Lawton.

Picked up from non-league football, Cunliffe played for Everton from season 1932-33 to 1938-39, scoring on his debut in a 2-1 defeat away to Aston Villa on 25th March 1933. Cunliffe would amass an Everton total of 76 goals in 187 games, 73 goals in 174 league appearances. He scored 3 hattricks at Everton, all at Goodison Park. The first hattrick came when he scored 4 goals against Stoke City on 2nd November 1935 in a 5-1 victory. He also second 4 goals against West Bromwich Albion on 11th April 1936, in a 5-3 victory. And his final hattrick came against Derby County on Christmas Day 1936, in a 7-0 hammering.

Cunliffe ended the season as the club's top scorer, with 23 league goals in 37 games, plus 1 game more in the FA Cup.

As for Dean, the broken toe at Anfield in the third game of the season was the start of another season of injuries. By now, the injuries must have been adding up, not just physically but also mentally, and Dean, still only 29 years of age must have felt a lot older.

There are many footballers who have given literally everything for "their" club, everything, sweat, blood and tears. Putting their body on the line time and time again. Dean was no exception at Everton, he literally was Mr Everton. He set a standard that the Everton supporters expect. He may well have inspired the motto of the club. If not, he certainly could have.

Beating Bloomer

Season 1936-37

Typical of Dean, just after he'd had a season of injuries, leaving some people to believe he might be coming to the end of his career, he came back on the first game of the season, and didn't miss a game for the first seventeen games, scoring twelve goals. In total he would complete forty games, scoring twenty-seven goals, and registering a goal in the first three games of the season.

Dean opened his account on the opening game of the season with a header in the 40th minute, in a 3-2 defeat away at Arsenal. In doing so, he equalled the football record of 352 career goals set by Steve Bloomer.

It was another goal from a header. Dean was more than arguably the greatest header of a ball the game as ever seen. Joe Mercer said Dean didn't just use his neck muscle for power, "He headed it with such force that you felt the power came all the way up from his waist."

It was another header that beat Bloomer's record, only a couple of days later, on 2nd September, in the second game of the season, at home to Sheffield Wednesday. The goal came in the 29th minute, in a 3-1 victory.

The following day, in the Evening Express, Dean was quoted as saying,

"Well, I have done it at last. I have reached the goal at which I have been aiming for many years and now a big burden seems to have fallen off my shoulders. It is almost impossible, of course, to give you a really true idea of my feelings at this moment. You see, I have been striving towards this objective for so long, that at times I am afraid I might waken and find it is merely a dream. I do want to say straight away, however, that it was the proudest moment of my life when the referee pointed to the centre of the field and I realised there was no disputing the legality of the goal I had just scored.

When I was a boy, I used to think how grand it would be to set up a new goal-scoring record. I tried to visualise what a football star must feel like. Now, I know that feelings one does get after breaking a big record. And I am almost too full for words. You want to know what it feels like to score a goal of this type? Let me try and give you some idea while I still feel the thrill of that precious moment. When we were awarded the corner kick on the left, I thought it might provide me with just the opportunity for which I had been waiting. So, I edged slightly to the right of the goal-mouth and quietly waited for Coulter's splendidly-taken kick to send the ball dropping perfectly into the goalmouth. Hardly ever taking my eyes of the ball, I leaped up and steered it into the net passed Brown, the Sheffield Wednesday goalkeeper, with a flick of my head. For a moment I forget everything. I could not believe it was true. When my team-mates crowded round, feverishly shaking my hands, and the crowd began roaring, and my old school-mate, Ellis Rimmer, the Sheffield Wednesday winger, also came dashing up to congratulate me, I Knew I had achieved my life-ling ambition....the roar of the crowd sent a thrill through me. You see, I have wanted to do this for years. It is 13 years since I scored my first goal in Football League match. That was for Tranmere Rovers. Ever since that day, I have had my heart set on putting up a new goal-scoring figure. Looking back, the time seems to have been short, although now and again it has seemed years and years longer than it actually was. It is when one gets really near to an objective that the energy and time spent in reaching that stage seems to tell. Last night, for instance, the minutes appeared to flash away and I was afraid I might have to disappointed myself and the crowd who had come to see me score the goal.

I have had thousands of good wishes lately from friends in all parts of the country, and I knew I had the best wishes of the Goodison "fans." I could not let them down. No, not any of them, especially the crowds at Goodison, where I have always received the best of everything in the way of encouragement. That was what I was thinking of mostly when I Led my team out on to the field for the match with The Wednesday. I knew they were all expecting me to break Steve Bloomer's long-standing record of 352 goals. And what is more, Steve himself told me not long ago that he would rather it was me who broke his record than anyone else. It is amazing what an effect a cheering crowd of 40,000 or so has on one's nerves. I was keyed up before I left the dressing room, but my goodness, by the time I had reached the field and was listening to the cheers of the crowds gathered all around the pitch, it struck me more than ever that I simply must not let them down. That was one of the thrills I received on scoring the goal. It gave me enormous satisfaction to realise that I had not let my friends down. I also derived much satisfaction from the knowledge that I had done it in Everton's colours, which will always rank first with me. Somebody once asked me which goal I considered the most important of my career. I studied for a time, but could hardly give them an answer straight away. Now I can I am certain that in my mind of any rate, last night's goal against The Wednesday's will always remain clearly defined in my memory.
Before I forget, let me disclose a little secret. Perhaps you will able to gauge my pre-match feelings when I tell you that I meant so much to me to break that record that I decided to do everything by the memory of it would forever remain fresh. So, after obtaining the necessary permission, I brought one of my own special footballs with me, and, therefore, as you will see, it was with my own football and not the club's that I scored the goal! It isn't often a player scores goals with footballs

provided by himself, is it? I did, though, and so you can see I have derived the utmost satisfaction out of my feat. 353. That number seems a big one. I can hardly realise I have put so many scoring balls into the net. But, however, big it is, I want to tell my friends that I hope to go on scoring for a long time yet. If I am going to retain this record for any length of time it is up to me to set up a figure which will not be overhauled in a few years' time. I intend doing that.

Now, I thank all of you for giving me such a square deal, not only on my own ground but on grounds in all parts of the country. And I thank Coulter for giving me the opportunity to beat Steve Bloomer's record."

In his next game Dean scored two goals against Brentford at Goodison Park in a 3-0 victory, and could have scored a third. With two goals in the bag after 24 minutes, Dean brought a good save out of the Brentford goalkeeper in the second half, before firing into the side netting when well-placed later on.

Dean continued with the odd goal here and there, scoring goals that helped Everton beat Liverpool, Huddersfield Town, and Wolverhampton Wanderers, and two goals in a spirited fightback against Birmingham in a 3-3 draw, a game they were losing 3-1 just after the start of the second half. Dean also rescued Everton against Stoke City, when 1-0 down with two minutes remaining, Dean scored from the penalty spot.

During this period of the season, Dean also scored his final hattrick for the club, on 7th November, in a 4-2 victory at Goodison Park against West Bromwich Albion. This was another milestone for Dean, as it was his 400th league career game. When the game finished, he'd now scored 362 league career goals in 400 league games.

His first goal of the game came in the 11th minute, from a long pass from Jimmy 'Nat' Cunliffe. The second goal came on 28 minutes, and in strange circumstances. After being pushed in the back on more than one occasion the referee gave Everton a penalty. Dean took it but the goalkeeper saved it, but in doing so it came back out to Dean who put it in the net with his head. It was reported in the Liverpool Echo as a "penalty header."

The third goal came in the second half, and another goal from a header. This completed hattrick number 37.

Although he only scored the single hattrick in this season, he came close to other hattricks in seven other games where he scored a brace. These included; Brentford, Grimsby Town, Derby County, Sunderland, Bolton Wanderers, Tottenham Hotspur, and Leeds United.

And as for injuries, the first game he missed this season was away to Charlton, on 12th December. The Liverpool Echo reported that, "Dean could not play owing to a damaged foot."

He returned the following game, and played ten games on the run, scoring eight goals. Starting with two goals in a 3-0 victory over Grimsby Town.

For the remaining eighteen games, he was in and out of the side, but still managed to play thirteen matches, scoring seven goals. A hefty challenge which resulted in a sore ankle and a penalty in a 3-0 against Sheffield Wednesday, kept Dean out for one game.

After scoring what sounded like a wonder goal against Sunderland, which the Liverpool Football Echo reported as, "Dean got the ball away out on the right wing, and it did not look as though there was a great deal of danger, but the Everton captain let loose a shot from fully 30 yards out –and from a bad angle at that –and the ball passed in front of Mapson like a thunderbolt and crashed into this far corner of the net", Dean was apparently rested for the next, with suggestions he had a touch of flu.

One game later Dean was back, scoring four goals in five games, before missing three of the last ten games.

For the season, Dean scored a total of 27 goals in 40 games, with 24 league goals in 36 league games. Once again, Dean was the club's top goal scorer, the tenth time in twelve seasons.

Although beating Steve Bloomer's record was another ground-breaking season for Dean, for Everton the ending of the season was a shocker. In the last fourteen league games they won only one game, drew five and lost eight. They were also knocked out of the FA Cup in a 5th round replay by Tottenham at White Hart Lane in a 4-3 defeat, were Dean scored two goals.

The only game Everton won in the last sixteen games was against Leeds United at Goodison Park on 3rd March, in a 7-1 thrashing. Dean scored two of the goals and by all accounts could and maybe should have scored yet another hattrick.

So bad were Everton's results at the end of the season, that they even lost twice to Manchester United who were one of the two teams relegated that season. The other team relegated was Sheffield Wednesday, who also beat Everton early in the season 6-4 at Hillsborough.

Everton finished the season in 17th place. They had the 7th best home record in the division winning twelve, drawing seven and only losing two games. Along with the 7-1 win over Leeds, the other two standout results came against Derby County at Goodison Park on Christmas Day in a 7-0 thrashing, with Dean along with Stevenson bagging two, while Cunliffe scored a hattrick, and the 5-0 win against Bournemouth in the FA Cup.

Other notably wins at Goodison Park included putting four goals past West Bromwich Albion and Portsmouth, scoring three goals against Brentford, Birmingham City, Grimsby Town, Bolton Wanderers, Sunderland, and against Sheffield Wednesday in both the league and cup. And not forgetting a 2-0 victory over Liverpool on 19th September.

But away from home, it was the same old story as the previous seasons, with only Leeds United having a worse record. Of the five teams that finished below Everton, they only beat one of them, Bolton Wanderers, and lost the other four games.

The disappointing thing was, and not for the first time, if Everton had matched their home record, they would have won the league with a couple of games to spare.

The Final Whistle

Season 1937-38

Five days before season 1937/38 began, the Evening Express reported that for the 7th season running, Dean was the club captain, and described him as "a fine skipper."
They didn't know, Dean didn't know, nobody knew, that this would be Dean's final season.
There was general excitement for the visit of Arsenal, and for the fifth season in a row, Dean scored the opening Everton goal on the opening day of the season, a headed equalizer in the 25th minute. But this would be the only highlight of the season in the Everton first team, and before the end of the season the curtain on Everton's greatest centre-forward would unceremoniously and shamefully for the Everton hierarchy, come down.
Arsenal, were the team that Dean made his Everton debut against at Highbury on 21st March 1925, and the team he scored his legendary 60th league goal against on 5th May 1928 at Goodison Park, so it was fitting that it was also against Arsenal that Dean would score his final Everton goal for the first team, on 28th August 1937 at Goodison Park.
Unfortunately, just like on his debut, it was defeat. This time a 4-1 defeat, against the eventual league champions and the club that not only tried to sign him when he was still at Tranmere, but undoubtably the most successful team of the 1930's. Arsenal won the league 5 times between seasons 1929/30 to 1938/39, and were Runner's Up on 1 other occasion.
After the Arsenal defeat, Dean played in the next two games, both away and another 2 defeats, 2-0 against Manchester City, and 1-0 against Blackpool. The defeat at

Blackpool was harsh, the team played well and should have got something out of the game. The Evening Express stated, "Dean was easily the best forward", and Dean was "working hard and using the ball well."

Unfortunately, Dean was involved in a crunching collision with Blackpool's Sammy Jones, in which Dean had some teeth loosened and a facial injury, which kept him out of the next game. In Dean's absence Everton won the next two games, beating Manchester City 4-1, and Brentford 3-0, both at Goodison Park.

Dean suddenly found himself in the reserves. Not surprisingly, Dean kept on scoring, and before the end of the season he would amass 16 goals in 22 games, helping Everton to win the Central League, and adding another medal to his collection.

Everton on the other hand had mixed results. Between Dean's last game on 4th September until he was recalled to the side on 23rd October, Everton played eight games, winning four, losing three and drawing one, with the highlight being a 2-1 victory against Liverpool at Anfield.

Even though Dean was scoring goals for the reserves, he was only recalled to the Everton first team on 23rd October away against Grimsby Town because Albert Geldard and Alex Stevenson were on international duty. Everton lost 2-1, and Dean was back in the reserves, where he regularly kept finding the back of the net.

Dean was recalled back to the Everton first team again on 11 December in the absence of Tommy Lawton who was injured, but it would be his last game for the first team. Everton drew 1-1 with Birmingham City, with Geldard getting the goal. Dean was described in the Liverpool Daily Post as, "a shadow of the Dean we have known in the past year."

Dean was dropped, back in the reserves and yet still found goals easy to come by.

Then the bombshell that stunned the football world was reported by the Liverpool Daily Post on 12th March that Dean had left Everton to join Third Division Notts County, after four hours of negotiations. They reported his transfer fee was the same amount as what Everton had paid for him from Tranmere thirteen years ago.

The Liverpool Echo were shocked and reported, "It is difficult to realise he is no longer an Evertonian." The newspaper also acknowledged that there was a reason for his departure, and they were unsure of the facts because the club refused to comment on it but they concluded, "the transfer went through because it was regarded as being in the best interest for all concerned, and not least of Dean himself."

The newspapers and the Evertonians who idolised him, hoped he would have stayed at the club until the end of his career, but it was not to be.

It was clear that the four-hour negotiations that took place over the transfer had something to do with Dean not really wanting to leave the club he loved, and he struggled with what he was about to do. But the overriding fact was, Dean and Everton club secretary Theo Kelly did not get along, and if he was to stay at the club there would be serious consequences for his actions that would surely follow.

Dean didn't feel threatened by new kid on the block Tommy Lawton who arrived at the end of the previous season. Indeed, it was Dean who met Lawton at Lime Street station to welcome him to Everton. The reason Dean left was all because of the sour relationship between himself and Kelly, a relationship that had become almost toxic.

Dean wasn't the only Everton player that Kelly seemed to upset, Tommy Lawton, Joe Mercer and T.G. Jones would later testify to that.

Kelly was an interesting figure at Everton, not only did he help to create the club crest, and become manager of the club in 1939, he was an excellent administrator who helped keep the club afloat during the years of the Second World War when Goodison was bombed. In some ways, Kelly was forward thinking because he believed players shouldn't be bought but should come through the ranks of the Reserves, and the Everton 'A' and 'B' teams instead of the chequebook. His downside was his man-management skills of the players, especially Dean and Mercer. To suggest Kelly was deficient in man-management would be an understatement.

Dean's exit from his boyhood club was a shock and a disgrace to the Everton hierarchy. For the whole of the season, with Dean dropped to Everton reserves in the Central League, they had declared officially that Dean was "not for sale". And yet, on Friday 11th March 1938, just days away from the end of the transfer window, Dean was transferred to Third Division Notts County.

Although Everton had spent the season saying Dean was not for sale, in the Everton minute books/ledgers, from the fantastic Dr David France Everton Collection, they show Everton receiving two requests for Dean's services, both within two months before he was transferred. In March, Blackburn Rovers wanted to sign him. Everton set a minimum fee of £1,500. This seemingly put Blackburn off. But more surprisingly, a month earlier Liverpool wanted to sign him. In the minutes, Everton stated, "It was agreed not to part with him to a Club in this city."

Imagine the backlash if that transfer would have happened? However, Dean would not have signed for Liverpool. He enjoyed nothing more than scoring against them. In his own words, "Anybody with the feelings I had for Everton was always dying to get on the pitch and get at the Reds."

According to Dean, Kelly was the only Everton official present when he signed for Notts County, and as the ink dried on the transfer paper, Kelly left without saying a word, not even a goodbye. Shocking.

Dean's last season at Everton, his stats were pitiful; 5 games, 1 goal. The dream was over and so was the tale of Dixie Dean's 37 Everton hattricks.

In Dean's absence Tommy Lawton became the next great Everton centre forward. In just over two full seasons at Everton, Lawton would go on to score 70 goals in 95 games, becoming the league's top goal scorer in seasons 1937-38 and 1938-39, and more importantly, helping Everton win the league in season 1938-39.

In season 1937-38 he would score in 20 league games from 39 starts. The following season, 1938-39, he would score in 23 league games in 38 starts. These included valuable goals in 1-0 victories over Wolves, Preston North End and Portsmouth, and helping Everton win the championship again.

So prolific was Lawton in the 1938-39 championship winning team, that he scored in every game of the first six games, (8 goals in total), and he scored 10 goals in 6 consecutive games between 8th March and 7th April. He scored 3 hattricks in this season, two against Middlesbrough, and one against Doncaster in an 8-0 victory in the FA Cup, a game in which he scored 4 goals.

In the two hattricks that he scored against Middlesbrough, the first was on 5th November at Goodison Park, in a 4-0 victory. Whilst in the return fixture he scored all 4 goals in a 4-4 draw on11th March.

He also scored against 18 different teams from 21 in the division that season. Furthermore, in his Everton career he scored a goal against every single club he ever against.

Unfortunately for Lawton, and for Everton, for the second time in Everton's history, a world war had begun and football was halted while they were champions. No one knows what Lawton and Everton might have achieved. He might not have beaten the goal machine that was Dixie Dean, but he might have given it a good crack.

There was a good reason the character Rigsby, played by actor and Evertonian Leonard Rossiter, in the 1970's TV sitcom Rising Damp, said, "If it hadn't have been for the war, who knows, I might have been another Tommy Lawton."

"Who's Tommy Lawton?" Alan, played by Richard Beckinsale, asks.

"Who's Tommy Lawton? Only the finest centre-forward who ever breathed, that's all." Rigsby replied.

After the war, when football had resumed, Lawton was no longer an Everton player, joining Chelsea in 1946. Ironically, he would end up at Notts County scoring bags of goals.

Dean's career at Notts County, on the other hand, got off to the worst start. After just 3 games he was injured, another chipped bone in his ankle. When he returned for the following season, disaster struck again after 6 games, and 3 goals, when he broke a bone in his instep. According to Dean it was his 15th operation.

Notts County knew the seriousness of the injuries and kindly allowed Dean to leave the club.

Dean would have one final swan song playing in Ireland for Sligo Rovers, scoring 10 goals, with another hattrick along the way (5 goals in 1 match), in 11 games, and helping to steer them to Runners Up in the league and cup.

And that was that, no more hattricks.

Statistics

In simple statistics William Ralph 'Dixie' Dean's Everton career lasted thirteen years and two hundred and sixty-five days. He signed for Everton on 16th March 1925 for £3,000, and was transferred to Notts County on 11th March 1938 for £2,000. It's often stated that the fee was £3,000. The Liverpool Daily Post reported that, "a fee somewhere in the vicinity of £3,000", but in the Everton ledgers it states, "It was agreed that the terms of the transfer of W.R. Dean to the club be modified and that we agree to accept £1,000 down and a further £1,000 at the season's end."

Maybe the local press was told it was £3,000 to show it was good business for an aging player, who although he was still an idol to thousands of football fans, he was nearing the end of his career. And the injuries were catching up with him. Not to mention the arrival of Tommy Lawton. Who knows?

Dean made his debut for the first team away to Arsenal on 21st March 1925, and his final game for the first team was at home to Birmingham City on 11th December 1937. During that time, he scored 349 league goals in 399 games, and a total of 383 goals in all competitions in 433 games. He broke goal scoring records one after the other, and created records of his own that will never be broken, both at club and national level. With one of those records he created being the 37 hattricks for one club.

For the record, of the 37 hattricks Dean scored for Everton, 30 were in the top flight First Division, 4 were in the Second Division, 2 in the FA Cup and 1 was in the Charity Shield. He scored 24 hattricks at Goodison Park and 13 away from home, at 9 different grounds. He scored hattricks against 27 different teams (another record), and on five occasions he scored consecutive hattricks.

He holds the English league record for goals per game, with an average of 0.867, and while at Everton he scored against every club he ever played against, with the exception of only two clubs, whilst in the Second Division (Millwall and Reading).

But Dean was more than just statistics, he was an inspiration to many a man. Even Madame Tussauds made a waxwork of him in 1929. When Patrick Anthony Connolly became an actor, he took his stage name, Bill Dean, from his hero. Born in Everton, Connolly would go on to star in films and TV shows, and was probably most known as the character Harry Cross in the soap opera Brookside. Dean was Connolly's idol, along with millions more.

Nick Walsh makes a point in his book, "Dean became so popular in the twenties and thirties that the nickname 'Dixie' came to be bestowed on countless number of males who happened to possess the surname 'Dean'.

This continued into the 1980's, when Alan Bleasdale wrote a character called 'Dixie' Dean for TV drama series, 'The Boys from the Blackstuff'.

There are numerous stories of people turning up to the gate and on hearing Dean wasn't playing simply walked away. Dean's pulling power and star quality stretched beyond Goodison Park. The famous comic/sports artist Paul Trevillion, testifies this when his father, for a birthday present, took him to watch his favourite football team Tottenham Hotspur in 1937 against Everton in the FA Cup reply at White Hart Lane. As another special treat his mum had knitted him a Tottenham scarf, "When Tottenham ran out in their white shirts, I roared my head off with all the other home fans. But then there was an even bigger roar when Dixie Dean took the field. He was such a famous star that everyone was shouting 'Good Old Dixie.' He was a powerful, imposing figure. Once I saw him, I was a Dixie Dean fan and I always have been. Tottenham were 3-1 down and came back to win 4-3 but I remember nothing of the game apart from Dixie's explosive heading power and the two goals he scored. When I got home, I asked my mother to sew the name 'Dixie Dean' into my Tottenham scarf. He became my hero and I wasted no time learning all I could about him and in later life I went on to draw him 100 times, possibly even more."

Dean inspires. He was the first Everton player to wear the Number Nine jersey, and in doing so he threw down a gauntlet. He paved the way for the romantism of Everton's Number Nine jersey. A jersey that was worn by club legends that followed in his footsteps; Lawton, Hickson, Young, Royle, Latchford, Sharp, Ferguson. But Dean's legacy had an effect on other centre-forwards; Vernon, Pickering, Heath, Gray, Lineker, Cottee, Campbell.

Dean's legacy acts as part of the backbone to the history of Everton football club. A club that were founding members of the football league, and with the help of the other eleven founding member's: Accrington, Aston Villa, Blackburn Rover's, Bolton Wanderers, Burnley, Derby County, Notts County, Preston North End, Stoke, West Bromwich Albion, and Wolverhampton Wanderers, helped to build and shape the game to what it is today.

Without these twelve clubs and the pioneers of the game, and the men who would become legends in their own right for clubs up and down the country, making and breaking records as they went along, who way back on 8th September 1888, kicked off the first season of professional football, then the glamour, money, celebrity, and development of the modern game would never have happened.

Footballers come and go, some may leave an impression on the fans that follow their football club, some leave a lasting imprint and standard, and other's leave a legacy that helped build that club and will forever be, none more so than the goal machine that was Dixie Dean.

The thirty-seven Everton hattricks Dean scored were in the following seasons…

Season	Number of hattricks
1925-26	4
1926-27	1
1927-28	7
1928-29	5
1929-30	1
1930-31	6
1931-32	8
1932-33	2
1933-34	0
1934-35	1
1935-36	1
1936-37	1

Dean scored a hattrick against twenty-seven different teams. These included…

Arsenal (1)
Aston Villa (1)
Birmingham City (1)
Blackburn Rovers (1)
Bolton Wanderers (Twice)
Burnley (Twice)
Charlton Athletic (1)
Chelsea (1)
Crystal Palace (1)
Derby County (1)
Huddersfield Town (1)
Leeds United (1)
Leicester City (Three times)
Liverpool (Twice)
Manchester United (1)

Newcastle United (Four times)
Oldham Athletic (1)
Portsmouth (Three times)
Plymouth Argyle (1)
Sheffield United (1)
Sheffield Wednesday (1)
Southport (1)
Stoke City (1)
Sunderland (1)
Tottenham Hotspur (1)
West Ham United (1)
West Bromwich Albion (1)

Hattricks in order of date, the competition, the team, home or away, result and number of goals in the game.

17th October 1925, First Division, Burnley (away). Won 3-1 (scored 3 goals)
24th October 1925, First Division, Leeds United (home). Won 4-2 (scored 3 goals)
12th December 1925, First Division, Newcastle United (away). Drew 3-3 (scored 3 goals)
24th April 1926, First Division, Newcastle United (home). Won 3-0 (scored 3 goals)
25th December 1926, First Division, Sunderland (home). Won 5-4 (scored 4 goals)
8th October 1927, First Division, Manchester United (home). Won 5-2 (scored 5 goals)
29th October 1927, First Division, Portsmouth (away). Won 3-1 (scored 3 goals)
5th November 1927, First Division, Leicester City (home). Won 7-1 (scored 3 goals)
10th December 1927, First Division, Aston Villa (away). Won 3-1 (scored 3 goals)
25th February 1928, First Division, Liverpool (away). Drew 3-3 (scored 3 goals)
28th April 1928, First Division, Burnley (away). Won 5-3 (scored 4 goals)
5th May 1928, First Division, Arsenal (home). Drew 3-3 (scored 3 goals)
25th August 1928, First Division, Bolton Wanderers (away). Won 3-2 (scored 3 goals)
1st September 1928, First Division, Portsmouth (home). Won 4-0 (scored 3 goals)
22nd December 1928, First Division, Newcastle United (home). Won 5-2 (scored 3 goals)

29th December 1928, First Division, Bolton Wanderers (home). Won 3-0 (scored 3 goals)
1st January 1929, First Division, Derby County (home). Won 4-0 (scored 3 goals)
28th September 1929, First Division, Portsmouth (away). Won 4-1 (scored 3 goals)
22nd November 1930, Second Division, Stoke City (home). Won 5-0 (scored 3 goals)
6th December 1930, Second Division, Oldham Athletic (home). Won 6-4 (scored 4 goals)
27th December 1930, Second Division, Plymouth Argyle (home). Won 9-1 (scored 4 goals)
24th January 1931, FA Cup 4th Round, Crystal Palace (away). Won 6-0 (scored 4 goals)
7th February 1931, Second Division, Charlton Athletic (away). Won 7-0 (scored 3 goals)
28th February 1931, FA Cup Quarter Final, Southport (home). Won 9-1 (scored 4 goals)
19th September 1931, First Division, Liverpool (away). Won 3-1 (scored 3 goals)
10th October 1931, First Division, Sheffield United (away). Won 5-1 (scored 3 goals)
17th October 1931, First Division, Sheffield Wednesday (home). Won 9-3 (scored 5 goals)
14th November 1931, First Division, Chelsea (home). Won 7-2 (scored 5 goals)
28th November 1931, First Division, Leicester City (home). Won 9-2 (scored 4 goals)
26th December 1931, First Division, Blackburn Rovers (home). Won 5-0 (scored 3 goals)
19th March 1932, First Division, Huddersfield Town (home). Won 4-1 (scored 3 goals)
16th April 1932, First Division, West Ham United (home). Won 6-1 (scored 3 goals)

12th October 1932, FA Charity Shield, Newcastle United (away). Won 5-3 (scored 4 goals)
8th March 1933, First Division, Leicester City (home). Won 6-3 (scored 3 goals)
29th December 1934, First Division, Tottenham Hotspur (home). Won 5-2 (scored 3 goals)
25th April 1936, First Division, Birmingham City (home). Won 4-3 (scored 3 goals)
7th November 1936, First Division, West Bromwich Albion (home). Won 4-2 (scored 3 goals)

Finally, that season when Dixie Dean the goal machine, scored 60 league goals...

Season 1927-28
27th August 1927, Goodison Park, Sheffield Wednesday, won 4-0 (scored 1 goal)
3rd September 1927, Ayresome Park, Middlesbrough, lost 4-2 (scored 1 goal)
5th September 1927, Burnden Park, Bolton Wanderers, drew 1-1 (scored 1 goal)
10th September 1927, Goodison Park, Birmingham City, won 5-2 (scored 2 goals)
14th September 1927, Goodison Park, Bolton Wanderers, drew 2-2 (scored 1 goal)
17th September 1927, St James' Park, Newcastle United, drew 2-2 (scored 2 goals)
24th September 1927, Goodison Park, Huddersfield Town, drew 2-2 (scored 2 goals)
1st October 1927, White Hart Lane, Tottenham Hotspur, won 3-1 (scored 2 goals)
8th October 1927, Goodison Park, Manchester United, won 5-2 (scored 5 goals)

29th October 1927, Fratton Park, Portsmouth, won 3-1 (scored 3 goals)
5th November 1927, Goodison Park, Leicester City, won 3-1 (scored 3 goals)
12th November 1927, Baseball Ground, Derby County, won 3-0 (scored 2 goals)
26th November 1927, Gigg Lane, Bury, won 3-2 (scored 2 goals)
10th December 1927, Villa Park, Aston Villa, won 3-2 (scored 3 goals)
24th December 1927, Highbury, Arsenal, lost 3-2 (scored 1 goal)
26th December 1927, Goodison Park, Cardiff City, won 2-1 (scored 2 goals)
31st December 1927, Hillsborough, Sheffield Wednesday, won 2-1 (scored 2 goals)
2nd January 1928, Ewood Park, Blackburn Rover's, lost 4-2 (scored 2 goals)
7th January 1928, Goodison Park, Middlesbrough, won 3-1 (scored 2 goals)
4th February 1928, Leeds Road, Huddersfield Town, lost 4-1 (scored 1 goal)
25th February 1928, Anfield, Liverpool, drew 3-3 (scored 3 goals)
24th March 1928, Goodison Park, Derby County, drew 2-2 (scored 2 goals)
6th April 1928, Goodison Park, Blackburn Rovers, won 4-1 (scored 2 goals)
7th April 1928, Goodison Park, Bury, drew 1-1 (scored 1 goal)
14th April 1928, Bramall Lane, Sheffield United, won 3-1 (scored 2 goals)
18th April 1928, Goodison Park, Newcastle United, won 3-0 (scored 1 goal)

21st April 1928, Goodison Park, Aston Villa, won 3-2 (scored 2 goals)
28th April 1928, Turf Moor, Burnley, won 5-3 (scored 4 goals)
5th May 1928, Goodison Park, Arsenal, drew 3-3 (scored 3 goals)

Bibliography and sources
Corbett, James, The Everton Encyclopedia, deCoubertin Books, 2012
Keith, John, Dixie Dean: The Inside Story of a Football Icon, Robson Books, 2001
Kelly, Stephen, Forever Everton, MacDonald & Co, 1987
Johnson, Steve, The Official Complete Record, deCoubertin Books, 2010
Liverpool Echo, Dixie's 60, Daily Post and Liverpool Echo, 2003
Roberts, John, Dixie Dean: The Forgotten Tapes, Trinity Mirror, 2008
Roberts, John, The Official Centenary History, Mayflower, 1978
Rogers, Ken, One Hundred Years of Goodison Glory, Breedon Books, 1992
Rogers, Ken and Cooke, Rich, Dixie Dean Uncut: The Lost Interview, Sports Media Publishing, 2005
Walsh, Nick, Dixie Dean, Pan Books, 1978

Websites
11v11.com
Bluecorrespondent.co.uk
Bluekipper.com
Efcstatto.com
Evertoncollection.org.com
Evertonresults.com
Freestandfilms.com
Toffeeweb.com
Wikipedia.org
Youtube.com